United Methodism in America

United Methodism in America

A Compact History

John G. McEllhenney, Editor
Frederick E. Maser
Kenneth E. Rowe
Charles Yrigoyen, Jr.

Abingdon Press
Nashville

UNITED METHODISM IN AMERICA:
A COMPACT HISTORY

Revised edition of *Proclaiming Grace and Freedom: The Story of United Methodism in America*, published under ISBN 0-687-34323-2.

Copyright © 1982; Revision Copyright © 1992 by Abingdon Press

This book is printed on recycled acid-free paper.

Library of Congress Cataloging-in-Publication Data

United Methodism in America : a compact history / John G. McEllhenney, editor . . . [et al.] . — [Rev. ed.]
    p. cm.
    Rev. ed. of : Proclaiming grace & freedom.
    Includes bibliographical references and index.
    ISBN 0-687-43170-0 (alk. paper)
    1. Methodist Church—United States—History. 2. United Methodist Church (U.S.)—History 3. United States—Church history. I. McEllhenney, John Galen. II. Proclaiming grace & freedom.
BX8235.U58 1992
287'.6'09—dc20
                                         92-4988

Illustrations by Ann Simon © 1982 by Simon Communications

05 06 07 08 09 – 14 13 12 11 10

MANUFACTURED IN THE UNITED STATES OF AMERICA

Contents

Introduction

John G. McEllhenney

One of United Methodism's numerous local churches gave birth to this book. Its rebirth occurred in another. Therefore it focuses on lay people, seeking to help them understand themselves as United Methodist Christians by telling them the history of their ancestors in the faith.

Questions raised by lay women and men guided Frederick E. Maser, Charles Yrigoyen, Jr., and Kenneth E. Rowe as they shaped this book's chapters, which grew out of lectures they prepared on the history of American United Methodism for lay audiences at the Ardmore, Pennsylvania, United Methodist Church in 1979. They transformed those oral presentations into a book titled *Proclaiming Grace and Freedom*, published in 1982.

I was that book's editor, and now, a decade later, as part of Methodism's itinerant system of placing pastors, I have moved from Ardmore to West Chester, Pennsylvania, where I continue to listen to lay concerns. As a result, I urged the three authors to revise their work by incorporating facts and insights unavailable ten years ago, and to extend the twentieth-century narrative into the 1990s.

The authors' original purpose remains unchanged, however, in this revised edition, titled *United Methodism in America: A Compact History.* They tell the stories of the Methodist, United Brethren, and Evangelical churches which now compose The United Methodist Church. They narrate developments in religious movements that stemmed from the evangelizing and organizing efforts of a host of women and men, whose earliest American leaders were Francis Asbury, Martin Boehm, Philip William Otterbein, and Jacob Albright. But since the spiritual momentum behind those efforts appears most clearly in the writings of John Wesley, who kept remarkably detailed records of his thoughts and actions, it is useful to begin with Wesley.

Wesley's life reveals that, more than anything else, United

9

INTRODUCTION

Methodism represents spiritual energy, the intensity of human willpower acting in harmony with the divine will, to bring persons to a saving knowledge of Jesus Christ and to send them out to reform their nation. Nowhere better than in the ministry of John Wesley can the pulsing physical, intellectual, and spiritual momentum of United Methodism be seen. To follow his footsteps even for a few weeks is to feel the drive that kept him ever on the move for God. So this volume opens by narrating two months' activities which highlight Wesley's utter devotion to Christ and the ceaseless breaking of new ground, which constitute the core of United Methodism at its best.

Wesley on the Move for God

John Wesley labored as an ordained minister from 1725 until 1791. But no period better reveals the moving force of his ministry than two months in 1787 when he was 84 years old. On Thursday, August 9, he crawled out from the covers at 4:00 A.M., his customary hour of rising, and took a coach to Southampton, a major seaport on the south coast of England. There the slightly built man (Wesley stood five feet three inches and weighed 126 pounds) preached at 7:00 P.M., delivering the first of 73 sermons he was to preach during the next 65 days.

Shrugging off the weariness caused by a tiring day of travel and preaching, Wesley arose the next morning in time to preach at 6:00 A.M. That early hour, before people went to work, points to his determination to fit his preaching into the schedules of the people he was trying to reach. Later in the day he allowed himself a brief diversion, listening, he tells us, to "the famous musician that plays upon the glasses." The following morning he and his party sailed from Southampton for the islands that lie in the channel between England and France. But when a storm turned them back into a port on the mainland, Wesley preached the next day at 8:00 A.M. and again at 4:00 P.M.

On that and the successive days during his two-month preaching tour, Wesley lifted up his principal themes. He reminded his listeners that it was appointed for them once to die and then to stand before God's judgment. That reminder, he hoped, would cause them to tremble for their sins. Then he told them that God had sent Christ to be their wisdom, righteousness, sanctification, and redemption. They needed only to respond in trusting faith to the preaching of Christ crucified. Following that challenge to trust God alone for salvation, Wesley exhorted his congregation to seek ways to continue growing in their love of God and neighbor.

After he had preached on one of those topics, Wesley and his shipmates caught favoring winds and sailed on to Alderney, the first stop on their visit to the Channel Islands. Before they could dock, they "were very near being shipwrecked in the bay," but eventually they anchored and, "though we had five beds in the same room, slept in peace."

Early the next morning Wesley, employing a typical evangelistic technique, sang a hymn as he strolled on the beach. Soon a small congregation gathered, beginning with a woman and two children, giving him an opportunity to preach. From the beach he went to a meeting with the governor, then sailed to another island, Guernsey, where he preached at 7:00 P.M. He devoted the next few days there to preaching, sometimes under a roof, sometimes under the sky. On Monday, August 20, between 3:00 and 4:00 A.M., Wesley's party sailed for Jersey, a French-speaking British island close to the coast of France. There his advanced age made Wesley a curiosity, thus enabling him to draw sizable congregations, which he addressed through an interpreter.

While visiting Jersey, he also finished writing for publication a sermon on "The Signs of the Times," in which he grumbled about church leaders who were not willing to herald the great work God was doing through him and his lay preachers. "Sinners," Wesley asserted, "have been truly converted to God, thoroughly changed both in heart and life; not by tens, or by hundreds only, but by thousands, yea, by myriads!" Yet the Bishop of London insisted that he could discern no special divine activity in the work being done by Methodist preachers.

Wesley, on the other hand, saw divine work in person after person. He noted the Holy Spirit changing the way people lived.

He also observed the Spirit occasionally offering extraordinary visions of God. On the island of Jersey he met Jane Bisson, who described an experience of "communion with the blessed Trinity, with God the Father and God the Son and God the Holy Ghost." While he admonished her not to allow her vision of the Trinity to make her proud, Wesley challenged others in the Methodist "society" on Jersey to imitate her pursuit of the fullness of Christian experience.

The "society" consisted of those who had responded to the message of Methodist lay preachers whom Wesley previously had sent to the island. Those who heard the message and desired to flee "from the wrath to come" were organized into a society, or small group, for the purpose of urging one another to keep Wesley's General Rules, which had three major headings: (1) to avoid evil of every kind; (2) to do as much good as possible; and (3) to use the means of receiving God's grace, such as private prayer, Bible study, attending public worship, receiving communion, and fasting.

Having examined the members of the Jersey society, Wesley began to think about his preaching appointments back in the Southampton area. But finding himself stormbound, he put aside his intention of keeping those appointments, saying, "It is my part to improve the time." He meant that instead of fretting about what could not be changed, he would use the situation created by the unchangeable weather to change human lives. He preached to the gentry of Jersey in the assembly room, a place that usually echoed to the sounds of dancing feet and rattling dice. Eager, however, to return to Southampton, Wesley sailed back to Guernsey. But the winds still refused to blow in the direction of Southampton, and he was forced to abandon his commitments there and sail in the opposite direction, for Penzance, the most southwesterly point of England.

Docking in Penzance, Wesley preached, wrote a letter to Jane Bisson, and began to visit the Methodist societies of Cornwall. A typical day found him, in addition to counseling members of the societies, preaching before dawn, at noon, and in the evening. Then he moved on again, arriving Friday, September 14, at the fashionable spa of Bath. The next day he sat down at a borrowed desk to catch up on his correspondence.

Wesley's letter to George Holder uncovers one of his constant preoccupations, the placing of his preachers. Back in the early 1740s, when Wesley's preaching had begun to attract huge congregations and to result in altered lives, some of his converts offered themselves to him as "sons in the gospel." These persons, not ordained but carefully instructed by Wesley, went out under his orders to preach the gospel. Now, at age 84, the placing of those preachers—appointing them to the circuits of preaching houses they were to visit on a regular basis—obliged Wesley frequently to take pen in hand. So he wrote to George Holder, telling him that he wished John Barber to move to Edinburgh with "as little delay as possible." That matter out of the way, Wesley preached in the evening on the first of his principles of Christianity, using as his text Ephesians 2:8: "For by grace you have been saved through faith, and this is not your own doing; it is the gift of God."

On Sunday, Wesley preached three times and read the service of Morning Prayer of the Church of England, of which he was a priest. For him, Methodist worship supplemented the worship of the Church of England; Wesley intended Methodism itself to serve as a spiritual reform movement within that church, not as a substitute for it. Therefore he urged his followers to attend Sunday morning prayers and the Lord's Supper at their local parish church; to share in a Methodist preaching service consisting of a hymn, scripture reading, sermon, hymn, and prayer; and then to participate in late afternoon prayers at their parish church, followed by another Methodist preaching service in the early evening.

After such a Sunday in Bath, Wesley rode on to Bristol, where he found his brother Charles. Certainly they talked about the way Methodists were wavering in their loyalty to the Church of England. Many resisted attending the services and sacraments of that church because some of the clergy did not practice what they preached. John mentioned to Charles the growing belief among Methodists that unworthy ministers prevent God's grace from flowing through the sacraments they administer. Charles reminded him that the Church of England, to which John regularly pledged his adherence and affection, insisted that the unworthiness of the minister does not undercut the worthiness of the sacrament. Thus stimulated, John wrote a sermon for publication, "On Attending the Church Service," in which he argued that "the sacraments are not dry breasts, whether he that administers be holy or unholy."

Wesley filled the days following his reunion with his brother with preaching, visiting societies, and writing letters. Three of those letters shed light on his mind and heart. One of his lay preachers, Jonathan Crowther, was short of cash. "You want money," Wesley wrote to him, "and money you shall have, if I can beg, borrow, or anything but steal." Next, he answered James Barry's inquiry as to whether Methodists ought to dance and play cards. "Possibly you may be saved," Wesley wrote, "though you dance and play at cards. But I could not." In his third letter, Wesley, an Oxford-trained theologian, emphasized his determined opposition to the theological notion that Jesus was merely an outstanding human being. No, he insisted, it was God who came to us in Jesus.

Emphasizing a divine Savior, Jesus Christ, for human sinners, Wesley continued his preaching tour. At one of his stops, Castle-Carey, he recalled that in earlier Methodist days, several of his preachers had been thrown into the horse pond there. Such riotous behavior had punctuated the first years of Methodist preaching, but now, Wesley exulted, "High and low earnestly listen to the word that is able to save their souls."

As Wesley preached in towns around Bath and Bristol, he also checked on the societies, talking personally with each member. Those personal conversations, like the conferences he held annually with his lay preachers, enabled him to assess the spiritual progress those people were making. Some he purged, having discovered that they were cooling instead of growing warmer in their love of God. Others refreshed the old man's spirit, "as their love was not grown cold."

Two more letters, written in late September and early

October 1787, open a window on Wesley's Methodism. He wrote to Henry Moore about a certain John Bull who was in prison because he could not pay his bills. "How far he was formerly to blame is not now the question," Wesley wrote, "but what can be done for him now?" It was not a rhetorical question, since Wesley instructed Moore to give Bull a sum equivalent to a week's wages, charging it to Wesley's account. He added that Moore should give Bull more "whenever you see proper."

Several days later he wrote to Hannah Ball, who was experiencing opposition when she, as a woman, preached in the male-dominated eighteenth century. "Some will believe your report," Wesley told her, "some will not." People who wish to be offended, he added, will always find some occasion for taking offense.

Time in Bristol now growing short, Wesley walked to the coach stop on Saturday, October 6, and prudently reserved the mail coach to carry him and his companions to London the following Monday. On Sunday, he preached morning and evening, and "took a solemn leave of the affectionate people" of Bristol. The next day, between 3:00 and 4:00 A.M., he went to catch the coach, only to find all seats occupied. When Wesley upbraided the booking agent, who claimed that Wesley had reserved seats for Sunday, not Monday, Wesley stepped aside, allowing his friends to speak "strong words" to the cheeky official. As a result, the coach company added a second London run that day. Twenty-four hours later, the weary 84-year-old traveler mounted his London pulpit and called on his people to "praise the Lord together." Then he "retired" to his desk and spent the rest of the week preparing articles for the *Arminian Magazine*, which had become a major source of information and inspiration for his Methodist people.

In addition to his editorial work, Wesley wrote letters, one of which demonstrates his interest in social problems. He addressed it to Granville Sharp, chairman of the British Society for the Abolition of Slavery. Wesley wrote: "Ever since I heard of it first I felt a perfect detestation of the horrid Slave Trade. Therefore I cannot but do everything in my power to forward the glorious design of your Society." Closing that letter, the old theologian-evangelist-organizer-social prophet turned his attention to the next Sunday, October 14, when he "preached in West-Street chapel morning and afternoon; and at St. Swithin's church in the evening."

Wesley's life—illustrated by the two months' events just narrated—reveals that United Methodism means that one should love God with all one's physical, mental, and spiritual energy. To be a follower of John Wesley is to get the good news of God's forgiving love in Jesus Christ straight in one's mind and burning in one's heart, and then go out restlessly, tirelessly, to share one's clear thinking and fiery conviction with others.

That Wesleyan passion for breaking new evangelistic ground impelled lay women and men to plant Methodism in Britain's American colonies. Francis Asbury, a key leader in America, stamped the contours of Wesley's highly energetic devotion to Christ on American Methodism. Similar contours characterized the early United Brethren and Evangelicals, the followers of Martin Boehm, Philip William Otterbein, and Jacob Albright. Their personal stories and the narrative of how the religious movements they created have now become The United Methodist Church fill the following pages, beginning with the mission to Georgia of John and Charles Wesley.

United Methodism in America

Part One

The Eighteenth Century

Frederick E. Maser

*The first attempt at bringing something like
Methodism to America, the mission of John and
Charles Wesley to the Native Americans of
Georgia, was a comparative failure. The brothers
left England for James Oglethorpe's Georgia
colony in 1735—John as a pastor to the colonists
and missionary to the Indians, Charles as the
governor's secretary. Back home less than two
years later, they were not sure they had preached
the gospel efficaciously; they were not even
certain of their own faith in Christ.*

Chapter One

Beginnings in America

1735 to 1773

The Mission to Georgia

John and Charles Wesley, priests of the Church of England, also called the Anglican Church, embarked for Georgia in 1735 as pastors to the colonists and, they hoped, missionaries to the Native Americans. They came from Oxford University, where they had formed small groups of students who regularly attended communion and gathered for daily prayer, fasting, frequent self-examination, and Bible study. Later they began to aid the poor and the imprisoned and to assist in tutoring the children of those people. The strict rules they laid down to govern themselves led other students to term them *Methodists*.

On arriving in Georgia in 1736, the Wesleys tried, without too much success, to force this rigid Methodism on the colonists. It is true that John fulfilled his pastoral duties. He taught the children and wrote a catechism for them; he published his first hymnal; he visited his people regularly and held services each day at 5:00 A.M. and in the evening. On Sunday he conducted the service at 5:00, read the communion service and preached at 11:00, and in the afternoon, read the evening service at 3:00.

The inflexibility with which the Wesley brothers carried out their religious practices soon alienated the majority of the colonists. John denounced the religious laxity of the people, insisting on plain dress with no display of jewelry, and attempted to implant his pattern of disciplined Christian living into a people who were struggling to adapt to a new and frightening frontier environment. He refused communion to one person simply because the man had not been baptized by a clergyman ordained by a bishop, and he had little sympathy for most non-Anglicans. He dipped babies during the baptismal service, sometimes against the will of their parents, and insisted upon rebaptizing dissenters before admitting them to communion. Both brothers naturally objected to hunting and fishing on Sundays, and both stood against slavery and the use of spirituous liquors.

John Wesley was friendly with the Moravian settlers, some of whom he had met on the voyage to Georgia. The Moravians stressed faith in Christ in terms of personal trust, commitment, and love, rather than in terms of duty. John admired their simplicity and sincerity of faith and often attended their meetings. In addition, he formed some of the more serious-minded of his own people into Methodist classes or small groups for prayer, Bible study, and mutual conversations about the Christian faith. Some of these groups met after the 3:00 P.M. service on Sunday.

Other factors, unfortunately, entered into the Georgia ministry. The mission to the Native Americans was unsuccessful. In addition, Charles Wesley, who had been serving as secretary to James Oglethorpe, the governor and one of the founders of the colony, resigned the position for which he was totally unfit and returned to England. John had a disastrous infatuation for Sophy Hopkey, the niece of the chief magistrate; she eventually married another man. The situation developed into a scandal when Wesley refused communion to Sophy because she failed to follow certain church rules. He was arrested and indicted on numerous charges, the most serious of which was the defamation of Sophy's character. Though he repeatedly sought action from the courts, he was never brought to trial. When he fled the colony in 1737, the first stage of Methodism in America ended.

In the meantime, George Whitefield, an Anglican priest and also a member of the Oxford Methodists, came to the New World and served in Georgia for a time as successor to John Wesley. He later became one of the outstanding leaders of the Great Awakening—a revival movement that began in the middle colonies, thrived in New England under the preaching of Jonathan Edwards, and then died down, only to be revived by

21

Whitefield and others. Whitefield went back and forth between England and America thirteen times, preaching wherever he went.

American Methodism Born in England

Back in England, the Wesleys, through the Moravians they had met, were led to a personal experience of faith in Christ, accompanied by an assurance that their sins had been forgiven. Both brothers enjoyed this deepening of their religious faith within a few days of each other. John's experience took place at a Moravian meeting in London's Aldersgate Street on May 24, 1738. It is better known than his brother's, which had occurred three days earlier, because of the often quoted lines from John's *Journal:* "I felt my heart strangely warmed. I felt I did trust in Christ, Christ alone for salvation; and an assurance was given me that He had taken away *my* sins, even mine, and saved *me* from the law of sin and death."

That experience, which emphasized the doctrine of justification, or salvation by faith in Christ alone, was of tremendous importance to the Wesleys. John began to preach with new power and confidence. Though the doctrine was not new to him, he had never before given it priority. Now he preached it so fervently that invitations to preach dried up.

Unfortunately, John's religious experience did not always reflect the confidence evident in his sermons. His faith at times was weak, and although he triumphed over sin, he did not experience the joy he believed should be a part of his new life. He even lost, at times, the assurance of salvation. This is not an unusual state in the experience of conversion and is reflected in the lives of many other Christians. For about a year he struggled inwardly to find himself and to understand the religious faith about which he was so confidently preaching.

During this time, conscious of his need, John went to Herrnhut, Germany, to study the Moravian doctrines and practices at their headquarters. He was deeply impressed by the piety of some Moravians, disillusioned by others. When he returned to London he continued to meet with various religious societies, especially the Moravian Society at Fetter Lane.

In the meantime, George Whitefield was in Bristol, England, preaching out of doors to many of the miners in the vicinity who seldom visited the churches. When he wrote to Wesley, urging him to come and help, John made the trip to Bristol and was greatly impressed by Whitefield's successful outdoor preaching, even though it went against the rules of the Church of England. The success of Whitefield, however, convinced Wesley of the godliness of outdoor preaching. So he consented to become "more vile"—that is, to break church rules and preach under the sky, for the sake of the gospel.

This was a critical juncture in the history of Methodism, not only because Wesley was laying aside church rules but, more important, because he was finding a way to reach the multitude untouched by the church. In addition, his rejection of convention brought him what his May 24, 1738, "conversion" had failed to give him—a steadiness in his own Christian faith, resulting from the discovery that God was using him to change the lives of a growing number of men and women.

But Wesley did more than preach. He continued his custom of forming his converts into small groups, or societies. These societies were composed of believers who gathered regularly for prayer, Bible study, and the deepening of their spiritual experience, and, when an Anglican priest was present, for a sermon. However, neither the Wesleys nor the people who were members ever considered the society a substitute for the church, where they received the sacraments and where they went for marriages, baptisms, and burials, in addition to attending Sunday services.

Wesley often stated that the only requirement for membership in a Methodist society was a desire to flee from the wrath to come, and a society member was expected to demonstrate a seriousness of manner in keeping with this purpose. In addition, members were expected to follow the General Rules published by the Wesleys. These included plainness of dress; doing good, such as helping the poor; using the "means of grace"; avoiding such sins as drunkenness, the selling of spirituous liquors, fighting, going to law against one another, returning evil for evil, and a whole host of other sins, even including "the singing of those songs, or reading those books, which do not tend to the knowledge or love of God."

Societies sometimes were divided into classes, with a leader who regularly interrogated each member concerning his or her spiritual condition, and sometimes these classes were divided into bands of only three or four persons. To be a Methodist in those early days meant being under the constant scrutiny of one's fellow Methodists and conducting one's life in accordance with the Wesley rules.

The classes and societies were closed bodies, requiring a ticket signed by a Methodist leader, for admission. However, under Wesley's guidance, the societies also held preaching services for the general public, in hope of making converts and securing new recruits.

John Wesley's message centered in a handful of simple truths: because of sin, persons need to be saved; by faith in the redemptive work of Christ, they can be saved; through faith in Christ, they can receive the assurance of their salvation; and through the Holy Spirit, they can become perfect in love, either instantly or by spiritual development. The change in the believer wrought by faith in Christ is referred to as *the new birth*. The fruit of the experience is a new life expressed in daily Christian conduct. And the believer was expected to use the *means of grace*—namely, attend church, say prayers, study the Bible, receive communion, and fast weekly. Wesley's message also centered on a large number of social concerns, including, at a later date, an effective opposition to slavery.

The new movement spread, and soon England was dotted with Methodist societies. When additional preachers were needed, Wesley, encouraged by his mother, began to select gifted lay persons to preach in the societies, many of which had rented or erected their own buildings. Wesley made it clear, however, that the movement was not a new church, but rather a renewal movement within the Church of England.

While Wesley's work was expanding in England, Whitefield continued to preach in America, but he never formed the permanent societies of devout Christians that characterized Wesley's work in England. His chief importance for Methodism lay in the fact that he prepared the ground for later Methodist work. Before continuing our story, however, it might be well to discover what America was like in the days of Whitefield and Wesley.

The Soil for Planting

By the middle of the eighteenth century, the American colonies were populated by a growing, bustling, independent people. Most of the immigrants were from northern Europe and Great Britain; by 1760, Anglicans, Baptists, Congregationalists, Dutch and German Reformed, Jews, Lutherans, Moravians, Presbyterians, Quakers, Roman Catholics, and a handful of small sects were on the scene. In certain colonies, some denominations had succeeded in becoming "established"—that is, a church supported by taxes. No one denomination, however, had been able to capture the entire seaboard.

In fact, by the 1760s, the Great Awakening, the name given to the religious fervor stirred up by the evangelistic efforts of Whitefield and others, had largely died down. It was followed by what one historian has called the Great Sleep. Only one person in seven belonged to a church in the New England colonies, and in New Jersey, only about one in fifteen. Farther south, the church members numbered even fewer, due partly to the demands of colonial living, when Sunday was the one day when a person might rest, enjoy some form of recreation, or go hunting or fishing.

It may also have been due, in some measure, to the rapid growth in population which made it difficult to minister to everyone. In 1650 the population was 52,000; in 1700 it had grown to 250,000; by 1760, to 1,700,000. In 1770 there were about two million people in the colonies; in 1780, nearer three million; by 1790, almost four million. These people had been

25

uprooted from familiar surroundings and thrust into a new situation where they experienced the feeling of being lost, which so often results from change. They needed the help and direction that religion can give, but they were not easily reached, and many were indifferent to the churches' message.

In contrast to life in Europe and England, however, a spirit of democracy swept the colonies. This spirit was partly due to the Great Awakening, which had proclaimed that *all* persons are sinners in need of a Savior, and it was furthered by the circumstances of colonial life. In the Old World, the family into which one was born was an important factor in deciding one's place in the world, but this had less importance in the colonies, where skill, flexibility, inventiveness, adaptability, and the willingness to work carried more weight than a person's coat of arms.

In spite of these factors, which offered a rare opportunity for Methodism, John Wesley did not seek to evangelize the New World at this time, and George Whitefield failed to organize Methodist-type societies in America. However, what these men failed to do was partially accomplished by a German Reformed pastor, Philip William Otterbein, who came to America in 1752. He was a preacher destined to evangelize large numbers of Germans in this country and to join forces with Martin Boehm, a leader of revivals among Pennsylvania German settlers. Together, they formed the Church of the United Brethren in Christ.

The Origins of the Church of the United Brethren in Christ

Philip William Otterbein

Philip William Otterbein was born in Germany on June 3, 1726. His father, uncle, and five brothers were ministers in the German Reformed Church, and his sister married a minister. He received a university education and was nurtured in a mellowed Calvinism which did not stress the doctrine that God predestined some to be saved and others to be damned. He was ordained in

1749 and became pastor of a German Reformed church. Because his forthright sermons disturbed his people, they were probably glad when he answered a call to serve in the New World.

Otterbein arrived in America on July 28, 1752, and became pastor of a German Reformed congregation in Lancaster, Pennsylvania, the second largest German Reformed church in America. Here he learned that forthright preaching does not necessarily meet everyone's religious needs. In 1754, after preaching a stirring sermon on God's grace, Otterbein was confronted by a man convinced of his own sinfulness, who asked about the meaning of grace. Otterbein shook his head and answered sadly, "Advice is scarce with me this day." He then went into his study, locked the door, and resolved never to preach again until he had obtained the peace and joy of a conscious salvation. Through a religious experience not unlike that of John Wesley, he did become convinced of the reality of divine forgiveness and the assurance of salvation. He began to preach with a new fervor, not only in his own church, but also in southeastern Pennsylvania and Maryland. In 1767 he met Martin Boehm, the man with whom he became co-founder of the Church of the United Brethren in Christ.

Martin Boehm

Boehm, of Swiss extraction, was born in Lancaster County, Pennsylvania, in 1725. He and his family were staunch Mennonites who traced their spiritual lineage to the sixteenth-century European reformer Menno Simons. In the eighteenth century, many of Simons' followers came to America and settled in Maryland, Virginia, and Pennsylvania. They accepted the Protestant emphasis on the Bible, but they rejected formal church organization and infant baptism. It was their custom to select their pastors by lot, and Boehm was chosen in 1758. He was naturally shy and found it difficult to preach. His sense of inadequacy drove him to a deeper prayer life and Bible study, through which he experienced forgiveness and received an assurance of salvation and Christ's presence.

27

Like Otterbein, Boehm began to preach in surrounding German communities, and in 1767 he announced a "big" revival meeting at Isaac Long's barn, six miles northeast of Lancaster. Otterbein, having heard of the gathering, entered the barn while Boehm was preaching. When the service was ended, he made his way to Boehm, clasped him in his powerful arms and said, "Wir sind Brüder!" (We are brothers!). Otterbein and Boehm joined forces in preaching evangelical doctrines which stressed holy living among the German-speaking people. They enlisted other preachers and formed a fellowship based, not upon organization, but upon similarity of religious experience, and by 1773 had formed societies in Pennsylvania, Virginia, and Maryland. In 1774, Otterbein became pastor of a German Reformed church in Baltimore, where he served for nearly forty years while continuing his work with Boehm.

The Origins of Organized American Methodism

The Lay Immigrants

Organized Methodism in America began as a lay movement. Whereas Whitefield and the Wesleys had failed to establish permanent Methodist societies in the New World, three laymen secured a firm foothold for the societies. Robert Strawbridge, an immigrant farmer, organized Methodism in Maryland around 1760 or shortly thereafter; Philip Embury, a carpenter and teacher, began work in New York City in 1766; and in 1767, Captain Thomas Webb, a retired British soldier, formed Methodist societies in Philadelphia and other places. By 1766 Methodism had also begun in Leesburg, Virginia, possibly through the work of Strawbridge and others, and by 1768 a building had been erected there for Methodist use.

Early American Methodist meetinghouses were usually very plain square or rectangular structures. They were either of log, brick, or stone, and not all had windows, though those in urban centers usually contained windows and a pulpit. In some, a

28

balcony was an added feature, and the seats, both in the balcony and on the main floor, were hard benches with no backs. Heat may have been provided by a fireplace or a wood-burning stove; women sometimes brought heated bricks, or small perforated tin boxes containing live coals, upon which they placed their feet for added comfort; in summer they brought fans.

In that early day, it is hardly likely that all Methodist meetinghouses followed the same order of service, but they generally followed Wesley's pattern: singing, prayer, a chapter each from the Old and New Testaments, and preaching. The singing and preaching were the most attractive parts of the service. Many of their hymns are familiar to us today: "Come, Thou Almighty King"; "O for a Thousand Tongues to Sing"; "Love Divine, All Loves Excelling"; "A Charge to Keep I Have"; "Jesus, Lover of My Soul"; and at Christmas, "While Shepherds Watched Their Flocks by Night."

Since hymnbooks were scarce and musical instruments forbidden, the hymns were usually "lined"—that is, a leader sang a line of the hymn, followed by the congregation, until the hymn was completed. In this way the participants soon learned by heart a number of hymns. And some of the itinerants were excellent singers: Robert Williams, an early Methodist itinerant from England, sometimes gathered his audience by singing, and Robert Strawbridge was considered "a melodious singer."

Strawbridge formed the first Methodist society on the Wesleyan plan in America. He had come from Ireland around 1760 and settled in Frederick County, Maryland. Having preached as a Methodist in Ireland, he not only continued this practice in the New World, but also built a log meetinghouse about a mile from his home—the first Methodist meetinghouse in America. He traveled throughout the eastern shore of Maryland, Virginia, and other places, organizing Methodist societies, and was especially useful in challenging young men to become preachers.

Elizabeth Strawbridge, Robert's wife, was not only a gracious lady but also a decided help in her husband's work. While he rode from place to place preaching, she kept their farm intact with the help of friends and also witnessed to her neighbors. She converted John Evans, sometimes called "the first known Wesleyan Methodist convert in America." His home, as well as the Strawbridge house, became centers for Methodist preaching.

Philip Embury of New York also came from Ireland, where he had been converted under Wesley and from whom he had received a license to preach. In 1760, Embury, his wife, and two or three of his brothers, together with Paul and Barbara Heck, sailed for America. It was not until 1766, however, that he began to preach. Barbara Heck, who prodded him to take that step, helped him gather his first congregation of five persons, and their first meeting was held in Embury's house. Later they met in a sail loft, and on October 30, 1768, the group, which had grown in numbers, dedicated a small meetinghouse in John Street, New York.

Captain Thomas Webb organized the Methodists in Philadelphia. He had been converted in England, joining a Methodist society in Bristol in 1765; Wesley had used him as a preacher in and about Bristol and Bath. Webb always wore a green patch over his right eye, having lost his eye in a battle in Quebec Province. He eventually returned to America as barrack master at Albany, a position amounting to retirement. Hearing of the work of Embury in New York, he assisted him by preaching and, later, by contributing money to the building of John Street meetinghouse. In 1767 he made his way to Philadelphia, where he found a small group meeting in a sail loft. Two of that group had been converted by Whitefield in 1741: Edward Evans, a maker of ladies' fine shoes; and James Emerson, probably a dealer in medicinal herbs and remedies, who had held prayer meetings for their group of serious-minded people from 1741 until 1767, when Webb organized them as a Methodist society.

The First Preachers—Boardman and Pilmore

As the work grew in Maryland, New York, Philadelphia, and Virginia, some of Strawbridge's converts in Maryland, and

Thomas Taylor, a trustee of the society in New York, wrote to John Wesley, urging him to send preachers to the New World. Wesley asked for volunteers, and Richard Boardman and Joseph Pilmore offered themselves for service in America. They arrived in Philadelphia late in October 1769, surprised to discover that Captain Webb was in Philadelphia and had formed a Methodist society which now numbered about one hundred. Pilmore remained in Philadelphia to minister to that society, and Boardman, who had been designated by Wesley as his chief assistant in America, went to New York. The men exchanged places frequently.

That pattern of exchange had been established by Wesley in England. He moved his preachers to new assignments, sometimes every few months, thus keeping them "itinerating"—that is, moving from one area of the country to another and from one society to another. The practice was called "the itineracy" and the preachers were referred to as itinerants. As time went on, an itinerant became responsible for more than one society—sometimes, in America, for as many as twenty or thirty, most of which had been established by a visit to a community by an itinerant preacher. These societies were linked together on a "circuit," and the preacher was termed a "circuit rider."

On his first stay in Philadelphia, Pilmore set about securing a new building for the growing Philadelphia society. After searching for a suitable meetinghouse without success, he finally purchased a huge shell of a building from a man whose son—described by Pilmore as *"non compos mentis"*—had purchased it at auction. It had belonged originally to a German Reformed congregation and was called St. George's. The interior of the church was not completed, however, until after the Revolutionary War.

The Methodists moved into the bare building on November 24, 1769, and on December 3, at a large gathering, Pilmore made an important statement of the faith and practices of Methodists. He pointed out that the Methodist movement had never been designed to make a separation from the Church of England. He also stated that Methodism was intended for the benefit of all, in

Early United Brethren, Evangelical, and Methodist preachers—frequently they were not ordained—spoke to people wherever they found them: on the docks, in fields, private homes, playhouses, courthouses, and taverns. But as soon as they made converts, they brought them together for Bible study, prayer, mutual admonition, and love feasts. It was not long, therefore, before church buildings were needed.

every denomination, who "earnestly desire to flee from the wrath to come." One could thus be a Methodist and still retain membership in one's own church. Methodists, he explained, had come to revive spiritual religion, to proclaim that Christ died for us in order to live in us and reign over us in all things.

Reinforcements—Asbury and Wright

The response to the leadership of Pilmore and Boardman was immediate, and in 1770 Pilmore wrote to Wesley in most enthusiastic terms about conditions in America, stating that there was enough work for at least two more preachers.

At first there was no disposition on the part of the British preachers to come to America. Wesley himself thought for a time of returning to the colonies, but in 1771, when five preachers volunteered for work in the New World, the two chosen by Wesley were Richard Wright and Francis Asbury. Wright was never very successful in the American work, but the choice of twenty-six-year-old Francis Asbury proved a wise one.

Asbury was a dedicated preacher with a firm grasp of Methodist principles and discipline. He was a born leader, and although not appointed as Wesley's assistant in America to succeed Richard Boardman until October 1772, he nevertheless took charge at once. He enforced Methodist discipline and expressed dissatisfaction with the work of Pilmore and Boardman because it was confined too greatly to Philadelphia and New York. It was through his prodding that the preachers began to spread out to other places in the colonies. Pilmore made a lengthy journey for Methodism through Pennsylvania, Maryland, Virginia, North and South Carolina, and Georgia. His southern journey began May 26, 1772, and continued until his return to St. George's meetinghouse in June 1773.

Pilmore's Southern Journey and Its Importance

Pilmore's travels were of great importance. First, he gave the Methodist people in America a sense of oneness with Methodists everywhere. Having been sent to America by John Wesley, he helped tie the Methodist societies to Wesley's leadership. Second, by his amiable manner and able preaching, he made many friends for the movement and organized a number of new societies, including one in Baltimore and another in Norfolk. He preached in churches, but also in a playhouse, under trees, in fields, in a courthouse, and in a tavern—wherever he could secure a hearing. By his evangelical fervor, he proved the power of Methodism's message.

At this time, he was second only to Captain Thomas Webb in helping to unite Methodism in America. Webb, by his travels through New York, Long Island, Pennsylvania, Delaware, New Jersey, and Maryland, provided the same service as Pilmore, but for a longer period of time. Later, Francis Asbury, through his travels, held the societies together.

When Pilmore returned to Philadelphia in 1773, he discovered that Wesley had sent two more missionaries to America: Thomas Rankin and George Shadford. Originally, as we have seen, Wesley had appointed Boardman leader of the American work; then he replaced Boardman with Asbury; now he replaced Asbury with Rankin, appointing him his "general assistant."

The general assistant—to use Wesley's term—was expected to carry out Wesley's will for American Methodism and, in this way, enable Wesley to supervise the American work closely and keep some measure of control over all that was done by the Methodists in the New World.

Chapter Two

Events Leading to a New Church

1773 to 1784

Thomas Rankin was a dour Scotsman, thoroughly committed to Wesley and Methodism. He came to America resolved to enforce Methodist discipline, such as upholding Wesley's rules and Wesley's insistence that no unordained preacher be permitted to administer the sacraments. He was primarily an administrator. George Shadford, his companion, was the warm-hearted evangelist and preacher.

First Conference of American Methodist Preachers

One of Rankin's first official acts in 1773 was to call a conference at St. George's, in Philadelphia, of all the Methodist preachers in America. Ten preachers attended.

The business centered on four important decisions. The *first* action united all Methodists in America under the spiritual leadership of John Wesley. The *second* action forbade the preachers to administer the sacraments, because they were unordained. This was directed specifically at Strawbridge, who was administering sacraments, and who continued, in spite of this ruling, to administer them until his death in 1781.

The *third* action stated, "None of the preachers in America to reprint any of Mr. Wesley's books without his authority (when it can be gotten) and the consent of the brethren"—a prohibition made necessary by the activities of Robert Williams, a Methodist preacher who had come to America on his own initiative and had been reprinting some of Wesley's hymns and books. This action was important because it brought the publishing business under the authority of the conference and was the first step toward establishing the conference's control over all future agencies of the church.

The *fourth* action served to tighten the discipline of Methodism. Only members were permitted to attend society meetings and love feasts, although visitors were permitted from time to time. Everyone, of course, was invited to attend the general preaching services. In addition, it was agreed that each pastor was to give an account of his work every six months. In time, this became the statistical report which is part of every annual conference in Methodism.

In 1773, membership statistics were as follows: New York 180, Philadelphia 180, New Jersey 200, Maryland 500, and Virginia 100; total 1,160. These members were serious-minded persons who desired to be a "peculiar people." To that end, Methodist men usually wore low-crowned hats and coats with rounded lapels; women wore plain black bonnets, no white dresses, no jewelry, no rings. The men did not powder or tie back their hair, but arranged it in long locks combed straight down; women had neither curls, side locks, nor lace. The preachers usually wore parson-gray suits much like the Quakers; but, wishing to be distinguished from them, they wore collars on their coats and used a variety of drab colors, avoiding only the brighter materials. The dress of the United Brethren under Otterbein and Boehm was as plain as that of the Methodists.

Worship services also were unmarked by liturgical elegance. Preaching was the high point of the service, and often produced converts, who were placed in a class for their spiritual development. These classes could be led by either a man or a women. Mary Thorne, appointed by Joseph Pilmore, became the first woman class leader in American Methodism, and other women were soon placed in this important position. Some probably also conducted prayer meetings, but there is no record of women preaching in American Methodism at this early date.

A significant work was being done among the African Americans. Jacob Toogood, a slave probably converted by Strawbridge, began to preach to other slaves with the permission of his master. An African American girl was a charter member of the society formed by Philip Embury in New York. Her name was Betty, and she was the servant of Barbara Heck. Asbury was especially sensitive to the plight and needs of the African Americans. St. George's Society in Philadelphia, in the beginning, warmly welcomed them, and in 1784 licensed an African American, Richard Allen, to preach. Pilmore writes of preaching to classes of African Americans, but only once does he suggest that they intermingled with whites. Usually, African Americans sat apart at the meetings.

At this time, possibly the most significant fact about Methodist meetings in America was the air of excited expectancy during the services that emotions would be aroused and souls would be saved. People seldom experienced disappointment.

Wesley continued to appoint preachers to America until 1775, when the strained relations between the colonists and the mother country made this impractical. A total of eight preachers were officially sent by Wesley, in addition to those who came on their own initiative, and for the most part, their work was exceedingly effective. In the ensuing years, however, a series of crises threatened the entire movement.

Political Crisis—The Revolutionary War

One of the crises which threatened American Methodism was the Revolutionary War. It was commonly known that American Methodism looked for its leadership to John Wesley, who supported the right of Parliament to tax the colonies. This in itself caused the movement to be suspected by the rebellious colonists. Wesley, who advised his preachers in America to follow a neutral course, did not follow his own advice. In 1775 he extracted the main arguments of Samuel Johnson's *Taxation No Tyranny* and issued them in a pamphlet titled *A Calm Address to Our American Colonies*. Unfortunately, to tell the Americans that they had "ceded to the King and Parliament, the power of disposing, without their consent, of both their lives, liberties and properties," was the surest way to alienate their allegiance and respect. As a result, Methodists in America became the objects of suspicion, and the lives of some preachers and lay people were seriously endangered.

Fortunately, a shipment of Wesley's publication *Calm Address* was burned at the wharf in New York by a friend of the Methodists who realized the damage they could do to the movement. His quick action tended to minimize the effect of the pamphlet, although many people, aware of Wesley's position, were suspicious of the Methodists. In addition, all the preachers Wesley had sent to America returned home except two—Francis Asbury and James Dempster; the latter became a Presbyterian. Before leaving the country, moreover, some of the preachers spoke out strongly against the revolution, and one, at least, distributed printed matter which opposed it.

Among the American preachers, attitudes toward the revolutionary cause varied. In Maryland, for example, a resolution adopted by the Association of Free Men of Maryland, stating that "it is necessary and just to repel force with force," was signed by a large number of prominent Methodists. On the other hand, Jesse Lee, a leading Methodist preacher, refused to carry a weapon. He supported the cause in other ways, however, by driving a supply wagon for his regiment and acting as a kind of unofficial chaplain.

In those colonies which demanded that their citizens take an oath of allegiance that included the willingness to bear arms, the preachers suffered keenly. Francis Asbury took refuge for about two years at the home of Judge Thomas White near Dover, Delaware, where the oath of allegiance did not include this objectionable statement. He fled into the swamps when some American officers came to Judge White's home, possibly to interrogate him.

Eventually the opposition to Methodism died down. This may have been due partly to the patience and sincerity of the Methodists under persecution, and it may also have been because of a letter written by Asbury to Rankin in 1777. In the letter, which some time later fell into the hands of American officers, Asbury stated that he believed the Americans would become a free and independent nation, and that he himself was knit in affection to too many of them to leave.

Persecution seldom destroys a religious movement; more

often, it causes it to grow. Although Methodism declined in the warn-torn middle colonies, particularly New York, it continued to grow in the South. From 1776 through 1783, the membership almost tripled to a total of 13,740, due partly to a stirring revival that began in 1776 on the Brunswick Circuit in Virginia and quickly spread to seven counties. Many souls were saved and large numbers were added to the societies. One eyewitness wrote, "My pen cannot describe one half of what I saw, heard, and felt."

The work of the United Brethren under Otterbein and Boehm also continued to grow. This may have been due to the fact that although Otterbein now had his headquarters in Baltimore, most of the work was carried on in the interior of Pennsylvania, Maryland, and Virginia, rather than in the large cities along the seaboard where the effects of the war were more serious. Nevertheless, the informal conferences held by Otterbein and Boehm with their preachers were interrupted by the conflict.

Spiritual Crisis—The Sacramental Controversy

Another crisis faced Methodism during the years of the American Revolution, caused in part by the fact that, with the coming of the war, many Anglican priests returned to England or went to Canada. Since the Methodist preachers were unordained, this meant that baptism and communion could not be provided for large numbers of Methodists. Some of the people and preachers believed that if the preachers were good enough to preach, they should be considered good enough to administer the sacraments. At one point, some preachers in the southern colonies ordained one another; but Asbury and the northern preachers were opposed to this method of providing the sacraments and looked upon those preachers as having left Methodism.

The matter was finally settled in 1780. After conducting a conference in the North which supported his position, Asbury made his way to Manakintown, Virginia, where the dissidents were meeting. They were led by powerful men, including James

Estimates vary as to how many people in Britain's American colonies desired independence when the Declaration of Independence was signed, but scholars agree it was a minority. Hence, leaders of the rebellion had to win over doubting individuals and convince the colonies, from New England to Georgia, to hang together in the fight for independence. One of their pieces of propaganda was the "Join or Die" serpent.

O'Kelly, later the leader of schism. For some time the meeting was deadlocked, and then quite unexpectedly, the preachers agreed on a compromise. The conference decided to resume for one year the former practice of not administering the sacraments, on the condition that Asbury would write to Wesley for guidance. It was not until four years later, however, that Wesley arrived at a solution to the problem.

Wesley's Plan for American Methodism

Through his reading of Lord Peter King's *Account of the Primitive Church,* Wesley became convinced that bishops and presbyters (ordained ministers) are of the same order and consequently have the same right to ordain, especially in emergency situations. And Wesley believed that the situation in America, far different from that in England, constituted an emergency. America had gained political independence and had established a civil authority, but "no one," he said, "either exercises or claims ecclesiastical authority." The Anglican Church, to which Methodists might turn for baptism and communion, had no bishops in America, and many of its American parishes were without priests. In addition, Wesley had sought to have persons ordained for the American work by Anglican bishops, but without success. In Wesley's eyes, therefore, the situation in America was an emergency that called for radical measures.

Wesley discussed the matter with numerous persons, including Thomas Coke, a keen-minded priest of the Church of England. In the end, Wesley himself made the decision. Early on the morning of September 1, 1784, at a private home in Bristol, England, Wesley, assisted by Thomas Coke and James Creighton, both Anglican priests, ordained Richard Whatcoat and Thomas Vasey as deacons. The next morning, they were ordained as elders. Then, assisted by Creighton and Whatcoat, Wesley "set apart" Thomas Coke as a "superintendent" to function as a bishop for the American work.

On September 18, 1784, the three ordained men set sail for

America, armed with documents and a carton of unbound hymnbooks and prayerbooks. The documents included Wesley's certificate of ordination which set apart Thomas Coke as superintendent; this is considered the basic document on which Methodist ordination rests. A second document was a pastoral letter from Wesley, addressed to "Dr. Coke, Mr. Asbury and our Brethren in America." The letter outlines the "uncommon train of providences" which led Wesley to act. It tells how Wesley came to the conclusion that bishops and ministers are of the same order, with the same right to ordain. Pointing to the emergency situation in America, Wesley writes, "I have accordingly appointed Dr. Coke and Mr. Francis Asbury to be joint superintendents over our brethren in North America . . . and I have prepared a liturgy little differing from that of the Church of England . . . I also advise the elders to administer the Supper of the Lord on every Lord's Day." Included with the prayerbook, called *The Sunday Service of the Methodists in North America*, was Wesley's reduction of the Thirty-Nine Articles of Religion of the Anglican Church to twenty-four.

Coke, Whatcoat, and Vasey arrived in New York and proceeded to Philadelphia, where at St. George's Church, they publicly revealed Wesley's plan for the American Methodist churches. From Philadelphia, they went to Barratt's Chapel in Delaware, where they met Francis Asbury and a small group of American Methodist leaders. It was agreed that a meeting of the preachers should be called, and Freeborn Garrettson was commissioned to notify all preachers to attend a conference during the Christmas season at Lovely Lane Chapel in Baltimore. Perhaps as many as three-quarters of the preachers responded and participated in the conference, including, some scholars think, two African Americans, Harry Hosier and Richard Allen.

The Christmas Conference—1784

The conference took a series of important actions. *First,* the Methodist movement was organized into an independent church, the Methodist Episcopal Church in America.

Second, Francis Asbury, who refused to accept Wesley's appointment as "superintendent" unless elected by the preachers was, together with Thomas Coke, unanimously voted into the office. By the term *superintendent,* Wesley simply meant that Coke and Asbury were to supervise the work in America, but the two men and most of the preachers present interpreted the term differently. Asbury and Coke were soon called *bishops,* a fact which displeased Wesley greatly. Asbury invited his old friend Philip William Otterbein, later to become cofounder of the Church of the United Brethren in Christ, to assist in the service of ordination.

Third, a book of discipline which outlined the purposes, goals, and General Rules of the new church was adopted, along with Wesley's twenty-four article abridgment of the Thirty-Nine Anglican Articles of Religion. The conference added a twenty-fifth article relating to "Rulers of the United States of America." The preachers had always accepted Wesley's *Sermons* and his *Explanatory Notes Upon the New Testament* as their doctrinal standards; now they added the Articles of Religion.

Fourth, the Christmas Conference passed a motion to stamp out slavery. Wesley had been an effective voice against it in England when he published his powerful pamphlet *Thoughts Upon Slavery* in 1774. Thomas Coke, on several occasions, had endangered his life in America by his forthright preaching against slavery. However, the rule was short-lived, being offensive to the southern Methodists, and the church later allowed individual conferences to decide the issue.

In other actions, the conference stated that the church's purpose was "to reform the continent and to spread scriptural holiness through these lands." It agreed on a position, later ignored, to obey the commands of Wesley during his lifetime, and it approved the establishment of a college to be named Cokesbury after the two bishops. It also passed a rule forbidding the preachers to use intoxicating liquors except for medicinal purposes.

Roughly a dozen persons were ordained as elders, fourteen as deacons. Elders were given authority to administer the

The organizing conference of the Methodist Episcopal Church in America was held at Lovely Lane Chapel in Baltimore during the Christmas season of 1784. A number of deacons and elders were ordained, and Francis Asbury was elected to supervise the circuit-riding preachers. Philip William Otterbein, co-founder of the Church of the United Brethren in Christ, assisted in the act of setting Asbury apart for his work as superintendent.

44

sacraments of baptism and communion and all other rites of the church. Deacons were given the authority to baptize in the absence of an elder, to assist the elder in the administration of communion, and to officiate at weddings and funerals. Both elders and deacons had the right to preach. For the first time in its history, American Methodism had its own ordained pastors with authority to administer the sacraments, for which its people had been eagerly waiting.

Two elders, Freeborn Garrettson and James Cromwell, were sent as missionaries to eastern Canada; Jeremiah Lambert and John Baxter were assigned to Antigua in the Caribbean. This meant that approximately ten elders remained to serve the thirteen colonies and the western territories. The result was that the deacons and some lay preachers continued the work of Methodism in their circuits, with the elders visiting the circuits every three months to preach and administer the sacraments. These visits, with business meetings presided over by the elder, writes Thomas Ware, one of the members of the Christmas Conference, "gave rise to the office of Presiding Elder among us." Later the office became what is today—the district superintendent.

The elders and deacons were, of course, expected to use the *Sunday Service of the Methodists in North America* in their work. In reality, this was more than a single worship service; it was an abridgment of the Anglican *Book of Common Prayer*, containing:

The Order for Morning Prayer, Every Lord's Day.
The Order for Evening Prayer, Every Lord's Day.
The Litany
A Prayer of Thanksgiving to be used every Lord's Day.
Collects, Epistles, and Gospels to be used through the year.
The Order for the Administration of the Lord's Supper
The Ministration of Baptism of Infants
The Ministration of Baptism for such as are of Riper Years
The Form of the Solemnization of Matrimony

The Communion of the Sick
The Order for the Burial of the Dead
Select Psalms
The Form and Manner of Making and Ordaining Superin-
tendents, Elders, and Deacons

Although the Christmas Conference accepted Wesley's
Sunday Service, it was soon laid aside by the ministers, who
desired greater freedom of expression in worship. Many stated
that they could pray better with their eyes closed than open,
which would be required by ritual prayers.

The attitude of the ministers and the churches was expressed
in the General Conference of 1792, which radically altered
Wesley's *Sunday Service*. The changes were not made
haphazardly, but with a view to meeting the needs of the people.
Wesley's thirteen sections, outlined above, were reduced to six.
Gone were morning and evening prayer, the psalms, the litany
and collects, Epistles and Gospels. Wesley's liturgical year was
completely eliminated and the word *liturgy* was deliberately and
purposely dropped. In short, there was no longer in American
Methodism a book of worship as ordered by Wesley, but a brief
section on "Sacramental Services," later called "The Ritual,"
placed at the back of the Book of Discipline. Here, retained in
altered form, were orders for communion, baptism, weddings,
funerals, and the ordaining of ministers. Even with regard to
those retained rites, ministers received freedom to insert their
own words.

Theological modification also appeared in the work of the 1792
General Conference. The traditional idea that a person is
regenerated, born again by the baptismal waters, was softened.
And there was a softening also of the Wesleyan emphasis on the
actual presence of the Risen Christ in the bread and wine of
communion.

It must not be thought, however, that the 1792 conference
rejected all Wesleyan theology and swept aside all order from
Methodist worship. Besides the rituals for the sacraments, the
Book of Discipline offered these directions for public worship:

46

(1) The morning service was to consist of singing, prayer, the reading of one chapter from the Old Testament and another from the New, and preaching; (2) The afternoon service omitted one of the Bible readings; (3) The evening service was to consist only of singing, prayer, and preaching; (4) When administering communion, the two chapters from the Bible could be omitted. Thus, order was to mark Methodist worship in all places, but lengthy liturgies and formal prayers were no longer used.

There were, of course, several reasons why the ministers preferred a more informal worship service. Many of them had been converted apart from liturgical worship and therefore believed that there was no need for Wesley's more traditional orders of worship. Others probably believed that prayerbook services were not consistent with a sincere and abiding faith, and may even have thought that the use of ritual prayers and services was wrong. In addition, many ministers served on circuits that extended far beyond the cities into the backwoods and frontier areas. There the liturgical prayers, with their restrained though beautiful language, would seem out of place. An extemporary prayer, uttered by a minister on his knees with his face turned heavenward and his eyes closed tightly in the intensity of his feelings, would more readily fit into the environment he was serving.

It must not be assumed, however, that the circuit riders were ignorant men totally unaware of the value of Wesley's *Sunday Service*. Rather they were people who understood their calling and the communities in which they were serving. Some think that the changes in worship were brought about through the influence of Asbury; but there is little doubt that whatever caused the alterations, the changes were indeed pleasing to the ministers and the churches.

A curious fact about Wesley's worship book for American Methodists is that it omitted the rite of confirmation. Theoretically, therefore, the new church had no ritual for receiving new members, unless the baptismal service were used for this purpose. The American Methodists used their own method. Those desiring to unite with the church were placed in a class, and if after a six months' trial period they were recommended by their class leader or the pastor who might have also been training them, they were received into the full fellowship of the church. A form for the reception of members was not included in the church's official orders of worship until the middle of the nineteenth century.

The new church continued to provide its members with occasional services. These included prayer meetings, held usually on Friday, either during the day or at night. Their purpose was to intensify the zeal of the members and to prepare them for Sunday. In 1791 the preachers were instructed to appoint prayer meetings wherever they could in the large societies. Later the prayer meetings began to be held on Wednesday evenings, to provide a midweek spiritual lift.

Another special service was the Watch Night. This had its beginnings in Bristol, England, where the colliers had, before their conversions, been accustomed to spending their Saturday nights drinking in the local tavern. Now the Methodist societies provided the option of meeting for prayer and praise. Wesley encouraged the custom, suggesting that it be held at the time of the full moon and continued no later than twelve midnight. Pilmore began holding Watch Night services, not unlike long prayer meetings, at old St. George's as early as Thursday, November 1, 1770. Later it became a regular event on New Year's Eve, when the people gathered to spend the last hours of the old year and the first moments of the new in prayer and praise in the house of God.

The Love Feast, another occasional service, has a lengthy history dating back to the primitive church. Not a substitute for communion, it was a time of close fellowship and particularly a time for receiving gifts for the poor. It was, as its name implies, a feast of love—love expressed in early Methodism by the breaking of bread and drinking of water or tea from two-handled cups passed from one worshiper to another. The order of service usually was hymn, prayer, grace (sung), bread distributed by the stewards, collection for the poor, circulation of the loving cup, address or sermon by the minister, testimonies by participants to their spiritual experiences, verses of hymns, spontaneous prayers, further hymn singing, closing exhortation by the minister, hymn, and benediction. Great emphasis was placed upon testimonies and the offering for the poor. The service was held about once a quarter and required a special ticket for admission.

Each of these services was marked not only by the usual hymns but also by special ones. The sung grace at Love Feasts was, for example, one very familiar to all of us:

> Be present at our Table, Lord,
> Be Here, and Ev'ry Where ador'd;
> Thy Creatures bless, and grant that we
> May feast in Paradise with Thee.

Another favorite of that early day is still being used:

> Come, Holy Ghost, our hearts inspire,
> Let us thine influence prove,
> Source of the old prophetic fire,
> Fountain of life and love.

For the Watch Night service, with its emphasis on new beginnings, they certainly sang a hymn which, unfortunately, has been omitted from the last two hymnals. The first verse contained these words:

> Come, let us anew our Journey pursue,
> Roll round with the year
> And never stand still till the Master appear!
> His adorable will let us gladly fulfill,
> And our talents improve,
> By the patience of hope and the labor of love.

A hymn for communion which we sing today was listed under the heading of "Inviting":

Come, sinners, to the Gospel feast,
Let every soul be Jesus' guest.
Ye need not one be left behind,
For God hath bidden all mankind.

The Methodist movement in America had become the Methodist Episcopal Church in the United States, and a new day with a new challenge faced both the clergy and the people.

Chapter Three

The Early Progress of the Churches of United Methodism

1784 to 1816

The Evangelical Association

Jacob Albright

An important phase of the history of The United Methodist Church began in 1796, when Jacob Albright began to preach among the Germans of Pennsylvania. The Albright family, of Lutheran background, had emigrated from Germany in 1732 and settled in a farming district of eastern Pennsylvania. Jacob was born May 1, 1759, and received the bare rudiments of an education, learning to read and write in both German and English. He was active in the Pennsylvania militia during the Revolutionary War, and in 1785, after his marriage to Catherine Cope, a member of the Reformed Church, he settled on a farm in Pennsylvania's Lancaster County and joined a Lutheran church. Because his farm contained valuable clay and limestone deposits, Albright founded a tile factory. The integrity of his work and his business ethics moved his neighbors to call him "the honest tilemaker."

When several of Albright's children died in 1790, he was led to serious thoughts about his religious life through the preaching of Anthony Houtz, a Reformed pastor who conducted the funeral services for the children. In 1791, Adam Riegel, a member of United Brethren in Christ, aided Albright in his search for an evangelical religious experience.

Having found peace with God, Albright began to preach among the Pennsylvania Germans in 1796. He first traveled in southeastern Pennsylvania, then north and west, and still later into Maryland and Virginia. His evangelical preaching, with its emphasis on the need for a change of heart and disciplined living, rather than simple participation in the outward forms and ceremonies of the church, aroused opposition among the Reformed and Lutheran people. On several occasions his life was endangered and he was severely beaten. Nevertheless, by 1800 he had formed three societies in southeastern Pennsylvania, each with a membership of about twenty. These were people who, in growing numbers, were a living protest against the formality of their denominations and were finding an answer to their needs in the warm fellowship, spirited singing, impassioned preaching, and strict discipline of the new movement.

Growth and Development

In 1803 Albright gathered his followers for a two-day meeting at the home of Samuel Liesser near Reading, Pennsylvania. "Albright's People," as some termed them, declared themselves an independent church, stated that the scriptures would be their rule and guide in faith and practice, and ordained Albright as their pastor.

The first annual conference of Albright's People was held in mid-November of 1807 at the home of Samuel Becker, with twenty-eight persons in attendance, including five itinerant and three local preachers. The membership numbered well over two hundred. The conference decided to prepare a book of discipline based on that of the Methodist Episcopal Church, and it adopted the name The Newly-Formed Methodist Connection. One of the most important actions of the conference was the election of Jacob Albright as bishop of the new denomination, a title bestowed by vote. Six months later, on May 18, 1808, Albright died.

After Albright's death the work was ably led by George Miller, who edited the first book of discipline of the denomination, adopted in 1809. It was based largely on a German translation of the Methodist book of discipline. Miller's biography of Albright played a major role in keeping "Albright's People" together after Albright's death.

Another leader, John Dreisbach, received his license to preach when he was seventeen years old. Largely self-educated, he was bilingual, speaking both English and German fluently, and had a proficient knowledge of the sermons of John Wesley. He was a gifted writer, administrator, and preacher, and Francis Asbury coveted him for the Methodist Episcopal Church. In 1810 he strove earnestly to persuade Dreisbach to leave the Evangelicals for the Methodists, but was unsuccessful. Dreisbach was secretary of the annual conference from 1809 to 1812. His brethren recognized his unusual gifts for leadership, and after serving as presiding officer at two annual conferences, he was elected presiding elder in 1814. It was in this capacity that he presided at the first General Conference in 1816.

At that conference the group took the name Evangelical Association. In two other important actions, the General Conference chose Solomon Miller as superintendent of the printing facilities that had been established at New Berlin, Pennsylvania, and considered a proposal to unite the Evangelical Association and the Church of the United Brethren in Christ. Nothing came of the move for union at that time, however.

The Church of the United Brethren in Christ

Organization

It is not always easy to discover when a religious movement becomes a denomination or a church. We have already seen how an evangelistic movement was spreading among the Germans of Pennsylvania under the leadership of Otterbein and Boehm. Preachers and evangelists of a variety of denominations were preaching with evangelical fervor and proclaiming salvation by faith in Christ. Although at times the Revolutionary War made it difficult, they came together for prayer, fellowship, and Bible study, and out of these meetings grew a resolve to hold a conference to see how they might be most useful.

The first meeting was held in 1789 in Baltimore, with seven preachers present, including Otterbein and Boehm; a greater number met again in New York County, Pennsylvania, in 1791. When they gathered on September 25, 1800, near Frederick, Maryland, the group had greatly increased, and they decided to formally organize. It is on this date and at this meeting that some United Brethren historians think of as the time and place their church was organized. They did not assume the name of a church, however, but called themselves the United Brethren in Christ. Otterbein and Boehm were elected bishops.

Later, Christian Newcomer became, with Otterbein and Boehm, one of the strong leaders of the new church. Born in Lancaster County, he had been a Mennonite farmer, and on his conversion, his friends urged him to begin preaching. Instead, he married and moved to Maryland, but in 1777 he associated himself as an evangelist with Otterbein and Boehm and evidently attended the meetings of the group. He was present at the meeting in 1800, and sometime later began to agitate for a firm organization. The 1812 annual meeting recognized and listed thirteen "authorized preachers," and the work began to expand. A better system of keeping records was established, and classes and societies were formed in increasing numbers.

Expansion

The leadership now included George Adam Geeting, Christopher Grosh, and Christian Newcomer. United Brethren work began to spread westward in Ohio, Kentucky, and Indiana, leading to the formation of a western conference. When preachers in the West grew weary of being ignored by sister denominations because they lacked ordination, Otterbein decided to act. Assisted by William Ryland, an elder in the Methodist Episcopal Church, he ordained Christian Newcomer, Joseph Hoffman, and Frederick Shaffer on October 2, 1813.

The first United Brethren General Conference was held in June 1815. By this time both Otterbein and Boehm were gone—Boehm having died in 1812, Otterbein in 1813. Newcomer, who had been elected bishop in 1813, presided over the conference. A brief Confession of Faith was adopted, composed of seven paragraphs; four were based on the Apostles' Creed and the remainder on the Bible. A Book of Discipline was recommended and a denominational hymnal approved. The eastern and western conferences were formally recognized, and it was agreed that the General Conference should meet every four years, at which time bishops were to be elected. In 1816 the first *Book of Discipline* was published.

Some Characteristics of the Churches

Doctrines and Practices

It is significant that Methodists, United Brethren, and Evangelicals all emphasized the doctrine of justification by faith alone, but insisted on pairing it with holy living, or Christian Perfection. The main task of the circuit rider was the saving of souls; not much emphasis was placed upon social concerns or politics. This is strange, since John Wesley believed that every saved person should be a socially useful person, which meant becoming involved in social action and understanding the political events of the day. In America, Asbury stayed clear of politics and the social order. His journal and letters contain almost no reference to the Revolutionary War, the War of 1812, or other political and social events of his era.

Methodist circuit riders taught the General Rules as set down by John Wesley. These touched upon social problems such as smuggling, gambling, drinking or selling spirituous liquors, slaveholding, and other practices. The only national actions in the political field occurred in 1789 when the Methodist Episcopal conference directed Asbury and Coke to extend the congratulations of the church to George Washington, the newly elected President of the United States, and in 1800 when the bishops issued a pastoral letter calling for legislation to change state laws on slavery.

None of the denominations had an educated ministry. It is true that during these early years each denomination sought to gradually lift the general standards of education among its preachers, and it is also true that the organizing conference of the Methodist Episcopal Church in 1784 voted to erect a college, Cokesbury, which twice experienced disastrous fires. Asbury supported the organization of academies in some states, but it was left to a later leadership to create an educated ministry.

On the other hand, from their beginnings in America, Methodists published the religious tracts of John Wesley and other religious material. John Dickins was appointed first book editor of the Methodist Episcopal Church in 1789, and he founded the Book Concern at St. George's in Philadelphia. Early in their history, United Brethren and Evangelicals also became interested in publishing.

The three denominations did not trust the laity sufficiently to allot them a role in setting church policy. No lay person was a voting member of either the general or the annual conferences, and no women were ordained during this period. Asbury looked upon women with suspicion; he preferred a celibate ministry, and although he could not prevent his ministers from marrying, he once made a sarcastic comment about those who had to run home every night to their "dears." Dreisbach, by contrast, was twice married and often spoke of how his wives helped him in his ministry. He had eleven children by his two wives and enjoyed a happy home life.

The men and women of the three churches still dressed very simply, and their meetinghouses continued to be plain, unadorned structures. For many years there were no organs or steeples.

Sunday schools did not exist in great numbers in eighteenth-century American Methodism. A Sunday school movement began in England as early as 1769, and Francis Asbury is credited with beginning the first Sunday school in America at Thomas Crenshaw's house in Hanover County, Virginia, in either 1783 or 1784. William Elliot, a Methodist, began a Sunday school at his plantation home in Accomac County, Virginia, in 1785, but progress was very slow. In 1791 the first interdenominational Sunday school association was organized in Philadelphia, with representatives attending from various churches, including St. George's. Two schools were opened for boys, one for girls. They met during the week, as well as on Sundays, and taught spelling, writing, reading, and Bible. One of the schools was housed in the New Street Building at St. George's. Their success was judged by how well they were able to keep young hoodlums off the street and help them into a useful life.

Splits and Schisms

There was a lack of democracy in the churches, particularly in the Methodist Episcopal Church. As a result, several splits that weakened the church occurred in the last decade of the eighteenth century and the first third of the nineteenth.

The first split took place when Asbury refused to appoint William Hammett, a British pioneer of Caribbean Methodism, to the Methodist church in Charleston, South Carolina, where the members were clamoring for his appointment. Asbury insisted on the right of the bishop to fix the appointments and strongly opposed Hammett's desire to remain at one church for a prolonged period. Hammett left the church in 1791 and erected Trinity Church in Charleston, taking a large number of Methodists with him. He called the new denomination the Primitive Methodist Church, but when he died in 1803, the denomination died with him.

The O'Kelly schism in 1792 followed a similar pattern. James O'Kelly led a faction which insisted that preachers should have the right of appeal to the conference if they were dissatisfied with their appointments. This demand is evidence of a deep-rooted dissatisfaction with the growing power of the episcopacy, particularly the authority of Francis Asbury. However, the O'Kelly dissidents were unable to carry their point, so they left the Methodist Episcopal Church and formed the Republican Methodist Church. Its greatest strength lay in the border counties of North Carolina and Virginia. Although O'Kelly's group drew between 15 and 20 percent of its members away from the Methodist Episcopal Church, his movement had lost its momentum by 1801. He changed the name of the denomination to the Christian Church, which soon began to fragment and eventually was absorbed by other denominations.

Methodist work among the African Americans, though generally successful, was also marred by schism. Richard Allen, a local preacher and a member of St. George's Church, Philadelphia, protested strongly against the segregation of African Americans to a separate part of the church during regular worship services. He and a group of his followers walked out of the church during a service to form their own organization. Allen was not leaving the Methodist Episcopal Church, but he was leaving St. George's. He purchased a frame blacksmith shop for use as a church, and on July 29, 1794, Bishop Asbury dedicated the building. John Dickins, an elder in the Methodist Episcopal Church, accompanied Asbury, and in his public prayer, asked that the place might be a bethel to thousands of souls. And the church was thus named "Bethel."

Allen looked to the Methodists to provide his church with preachers and to assist in drawing up a charter. But later, fearing that the Methodist form of charter could be used to take the church from him, he had the charter rewritten. Tensions grew between Allen and the preachers at St. George's, and following a court action, Bethel was sustained by the courts as an independent church.

Hearing of discrimination against African Americans in other places, in 1816 Allen issued a call to those churches to form an ecclesiastical pact. Representatives arrived from a number of cities, and out of that meeting came the African Methodist Episcopal Church, with Richard Allen as its first bishop. The new church's first *Book of Discipline,* published in 1817, was patterned largely after that of the Methodist Episcopal Church.

Many African Americans remained faithful to the Methodist Episcopal Church. Some, like Allen, walked out of St. George's, but remained faithful to the mother church and formed churches within the framework of the Methodist Episcopal Church. The

John Wesley planted opposition to slavery deep in Methodism. Writing just days before he died to William Wilberforce, British anti-slave-trade advocate, Wesley said, "Go on, in the name of God, and in the power of his might, till even American slavery, the vilest that ever saw the sun, shall vanish before it." The 1784 Discipline of the Methodist Episcopal Church, following Wesley's lead, gave Methodists two choices: free their slaves or leave the church.

oldest of these is Zoar United Methodist Church, Philadelphia, founded in 1794.

During this period two other African American denominations were organized—the African Methodist Episcopal Zion Church and the Union Church of Africans. Members of the former came from churches in New Haven, Philadelphia, Long Island, and New York; it was organized in 1821, with James Varick as the church's first bishop.

The Union Church of Africans, led by Peter Spencer, began in Wilmington, Delaware, the result of a split from the Methodist Episcopal Church at Wilmington. On September 18, 1813, Spencer organized his followers and other groups into the Union Church of African Members, the first separate African American denomination in America. Spencer could not be persuaded by Richard Allen to merge with the African Methodist Episcopal Church in 1816.

The Churches Take Shape

By the beginning of the nineteenth century, the Methodists, Evangelicals, and United Brethren had made the transition from religious movements into organized churches, with ordained clergy, liturgies, hymnbooks, doctrinal standards, and books of discipline.

When the Methodist Episcopal Church was organized in 1784, it comprised local societies or individual churches, which in turn were divided into classes or small groups for spiritual growth. Local churches were governed by quarterly conferences, over which a presiding elder, or district superintendent, presided. The churches, through their pastors, were part of a larger body termed an annual conference. A bishop presided at the annual conference and ended the sessions by telling the pastors which churches they were to serve during the coming year. When the United Brethren and the Evangelicals organized, they followed the basic pattern of the Methodists, although each church had distinctive ways of handling bishops, district superintendents, and ordained ministers.

THE EARLY PROGRESS (1784–1816)

Every four years after 1792, the preachers in the Methodist Episcopal Church gathered for a General Conference, the highest legislative body of the church. The first General Conference of the United Brethren was held in 1815, and the first in the Evangelical Association in 1816. In 1808, the Methodist Episcopal Church decided that the General Conference should be a delegated body, with clergy representatives from each annual conference. In the Church of the United Brethren, this was done at the first General Conference in 1815, but it was not a practice in the Evangelical Association until 1839.

In 1808, the Methodist General Conference adopted a constitution for the church that included six restrictive rules. The most important restrictions made it impossible for the General Conference to alter the doctrines of the church, to do away with the episcopacy, or to appropriate publishing profits for any purpose other than that of providing benefits for retired preachers and their families.

In 1815, the General Conference of the United Brethren Church provided for the election of bishops with a term of four years, but with the opportunity for reelection; provided for one ordination, that of elder; and expressly forbade the General Conference from taking any action "which shall abolish or do away with the itinerant plan."

Unfortunately, none of the churches did much work among the Native Americans. In 1789 only three Native Americans were recorded as members of the Methodist Episcopal Church. In that year Thomas Coke resolved to carry on a mission among them, but never successfully pursued his goal. Methodists did not begin a ministry among Native Americans until 1815 or 1816, when John Stewart, a man of mixed ancestry, began missionary activity among the Wyandot Indians in Ohio.

During those years attempts were made at union between the Methodist Episcopal and the United Brethren churches, and between the Evangelicals and the United Brethren, but nothing came of these efforts at that time.

Worship in Evangelical, United Brethren, and Methodist churches during the nineteenth century owed much to camp meetings. It was informal and spirited, often highly emotional, with emphasis placed on fiery preaching, extemporaneous praying, joyful singing, and passionate testifying. People responded to such services by rolling, twitching, fainting, and making commitments to Christ that issued in transformed living.

THE EARLY PROGRESS (1784–1816)

Camp Meetings and Revivalism

At the turn of the century, camp meetings emerged, one being held in Kentucky in 1800, during July. The moving spirits were two brothers, John and William McGee, the former a Methodist local preacher, the latter a Presbyterian clergyman. Spreading rapidly, the movement was quickly systematized into orderly gatherings; people lived in tents or wagons, with supervisors always at hand to protect the congregation from intruders and maintain a high level of morality among the participants. The meetings sometimes lasted for several weeks and provided fellowship and religious teaching for vast numbers of people. They were often highly emotional gatherings; sometimes people fainted; some got the "shakes"; many experienced conversion.

The camp meeting reflected and counteracted the wild, carefree, explosive manner of living that prevailed on the frontier. It focused on the conversion of many people at one time; the older more traditional approach, that of one person telling another about Christ, would have made little or no impact on frontier communities. From letters and journals of the day, we learn that the camps were usually on a large tableland, cleared in the center and surrounded by trees. In the cleared area, hard benches without backs faced a high pulpit at one end. In some cases, smaller pulpits were strategically placed far away from the first, so that those who could not hear the first could be challenged by one being preached at the same time as the one in the main gathering. Soon people were shouting for forgiveness of their sins; many openly wept, and others danced for joy in their newfound salvation.

Throughout the meetings, hymns directed at stirring the fears and emotions of the congregation were sung. While they might have agreed with the general theology of the hymns, John and Charles Wesley probably would have shuddered at the way some hymns portrayed the Methodist message:

> Stop, poor sinner, stop and think,
> Before you further go;

Can you sport upon the brink
Of everlasting woe?
Hell beneath is gaping wide,
Vengeance waits the dread command,
Soon will stop your sport and pride,
And sink you with the damned.

To this was added a chorus:

Then be entreated now to stop,
For unless you warning take,
'Ere you are aware you'll drop
Into a burning lake.

Some hymns centered on Bible stories, presenting them in a bizarre fashion. A nineteen-verse hymn that tells the story of Daniel in the lions' den proved a great favorite among camp-meeting singers.

It was at night that the meeting took on its most solemn aspect. One writer states:

At night the whole scene was awfully sublime. The ranges of tents, the fires reflecting light amidst the branches of the forest trees; the candles and lamps illuminating the ground; hundreds moving to and fro with torches like Gideon's army; the sound of exhortation, singing, praying, and rejoicing rising from various parts of the encampment; all this was enough to enlist the feelings and absorb the powers of the mind.

Last Days of Otterbein, Boehm, and Asbury

Jacob Albright died May 18, 1808; Martin Boehm died March 23, 1812, after a six-day illness. Francis Asbury, in response to a strong inner prompting, had been on his way to visit Boehm when he received word of his death.

Otterbein died peacefully in Baltimore on November 17, 1813. When he heard of Otterbein's passing, Asbury said, "Great and good man of God! An honor to his church and country. One of the greatest scholars and divines that ever came to America, or born in it."

Asbury died on Sunday afternoon, March 31, 1816, while trying, in a delirium, to receive a missionary offering. Thus the four great early leaders of the Methodists, Evangelicals, and United Brethren died within a decade.

The first epoch in the history of the Methodist Episcopal Church, the Church of the United Brethren in Christ, and the Evangelical Association had come to a close. The growth, expansion, and gains of the churches had been remarkable. Evangelistic fervor was at a great height, and in 1814, with the closing of the War of 1812 and the opening of the West, a new era was beginning for the churches. The future held hope and challenge. The churches were on the march.

Part Two

The Nineteenth Century

Charles Yrigoyen, Jr.

Chapter Four

Growth and Development

1816 to 1843

The first half of the nineteenth century provided the opportunity for the American people to acquire an appreciation for the potential of their land, its resources, and the talents of its populace. When Francis Asbury died in 1816, the young nation was just beginning to realize its promise. It was entering a period of territorial expansion, agricultural and industrial development, and population growth.

The land was suitable for successful farming and abundant with raw materials for manufacturing. Inventions and improvements in existing machinery and tools resulted in larger productivity on farms and in factories. The invention of the steel plow, the reaper, and the thresher represented major advances in agricultural technology. The creation of the telegraph and the harnessing of water and steam power also proved significant for the nation's life. Canals, turnpikes, railroads, and steamboats opened routes for settlers, travelers, and goods.

Despite the financial panics of 1819 and 1837, the nation was progressing. Its people were optimistic. It was the age of the Monroe Doctrine, which warned European powers that the western hemisphere was no longer open to their colonization, and Jacksonian democracy, which provided for broader participation by the American people in their political life. Immigration from England and Europe rose dramatically. The population grew from nine million in 1815 to more than twenty-three million in 1850. For the adventuresome, there was a seemingly limitless frontier to explore and settle. The American people were developing a positive attitude about themselves, their role as a national power, and their future.

GROWTH AND DEVELOPMENT (1816–1843)

The Second Great Awakening and Social Reform

The most prominent religious development in early nine-teenth-century America was the Second Great Awakening. This movement of religious fervor spread across the nation, reaching its midpoint about the time of Asbury's death. While its intensity and accompanying phenomena varied in different sections of the nation, its major thrust was to convert sinners. In revivals and camp meetings throughout the country, there was an unprece-dented effort to bring the wayward to an experience of salvation.

Thousands of people, under the direction of preachers and lay leaders, experienced conversion. This transformation usually consisted of four stages. *First,* the prospect became convinced of his or her guilt as a sinner. *Second,* there was a feeling of despair; the sinner deserved God's wrathful punishment. *Third,* there was hope. God was gracious. The Holy One was always ready to forgive the penitent sinner and to restore the sinner to a proper relationship with God through faith in Christ. *Finally,* there was an experience of assurance. Guilt, despair, and hope gave way to the joy of salvation experienced in the sinner's life. This type of conversion was the goal of the revival and the camp meeting.

There were several important consequences of the Second Awakening. It stirred theological disagreement. Some vehe-mently criticized it as superficial, individualistic, and excessively emotional. Some critics preferred a more reasoned religion. Others disliked the new revivalistic techniques associated with it; they desired more traditional and formal religious expression. Pro-revivalist and anti-revivalist parties were formed in some denominations. Churches historically sympathetic to an experi-ential approach to Christianity, such as the Methodists, the Evangelical Association, and the United Brethren in Christ, witnessed remarkable growth in conversions, membership, and new congregations. Other American Protestant bodies, notably the Presbyterians and Baptists, also grew rapidly during the high tide of the movement.

But the Awakening envisioned more than converted individu-als; it aimed to reform society as well. Hoping to Christianize every aspect of American life, evangelical Protestants organized voluntary societies to attack the social evils of the young nation. These societies sprang up wherever interest in their cause could be created, and their memberships were constituted without regard for an individual's denominational affiliation. They were often effectively organized into local, state, and national structures; in conventions and rallies, and through the publication and distribution of literature, they attempted to mold public opinion and governmental policy in accordance with their reforms. Temperance groups which encouraged people to abstain totally from alcoholic beverages, Bible and tract societies, benevolent associations to aid the poor, women's rights organizations, abolitionist societies which intended to eliminate the scourge of slavery—these were but a few of the components of this "moral militia." Many Protestants believed that the dream of the Puritan forebears of a Christian America was soon to be realized, and revivalism and social reform were the means by which it would be attained. The spiritual kin of the Wesleys, Albright, and Otterbein were eager to work for its attainment.

Keys to Continued Growth

The years 1816 through 1843 were marked by significant growth in each of the churches that currently compose United Methodism. Methodists numbered about one million by 1843; the Evangelical Association reported more than a 500 percent increase in members; the United Brethren likewise witnessed a large rise in membership. The churches could boast also about the establishment of new congregations and swelling ministerial ranks. How can we account for this extraordinary growth? Several factors may explain it. Among the most important are the unusual dedication of the preachers and the laity, a form of organization suited to the conditions of the time, and the extension of the ministries of the Evangelical Association and the United Brethren Church to English-speaking people.

Dedication

Virtually all the preachers in these churches were convinced that they were called of God. This call came to them in a variety of ways, and it was the principal motivation for their ministry in settled communities or sparsely settled frontier areas. Those who answered the call were soon aware that theirs was a demanding and disciplined vocation. They were expected to preach, organize classes, visit the sick, stir up the weak in faith, encourage and support the faithful, read and study the scriptures and other edifying literature, and set an example for the laity. Many preachers, particularly on the frontier, often were required to function in severely adverse geographical and weather conditions. Furthermore, many encountered hostility from those belonging to other churches who resented their theology and methods, as well as from unbelievers who were equally antagonistic.

The work was demanding, the wages modest. In 1816 the preachers of the Evangelical Association were paid $60 per year, plus travel expenses; as late as 1843, their annual wage was $100 if single, $200 if married, with an additional $25 for each child under fourteen years of age. Salaries among the Methodists and United Brethren were comparable. Many of the clergy supplemented their income by acting as agents for the sale of books and literature from their publishing houses, but even this resulted in very little additional revenue. Among the earlier preachers, marriage was discouraged because of the low wages and the extended absences caused by riding a circuit.

Rigid standards of conduct for the laity were enforced in the churches. Methodism had formulated rigorous principles for both clergy and laity in the General Rules adopted at the Christmas Conference in 1784. Methodists were urged to do no harm and to avoid evil of every kind. Included in this prohibition were profaning the sabbath, drunkenness, wearing gold and costly apparel, fighting and quarreling, singing songs and reading books that did not lead to the knowledge and love of God, and "laying up treasures upon earth." They were also expected to

71

do good: Feeding the hungry, clothing the naked, visiting the sick and imprisoned, "denying themselves, and taking up their cross daily," were among the positive disciplines Methodists were to practice. They were also required to observe "all the ordinances of God," such as attendance at public worship and the Lord's Supper, private prayer, fasting, and Bible study. Similar standards probably kept membership lower than it otherwise might have been among the Evangelicals and the United Brethren. The laity, as much as the clergy, were expected to be converted, committed, and disciplined participants in the churches to which they belonged. Together, they rejoiced in a fellowship that was mutually beneficial.

Organization

A second important factor in the expansion of the churches was the manner in which they were organized. The Wesleyan model of small groups called classes was especially useful in rural and frontier regions. Classes ranged in membership from three or four persons up to fifty or more. Each class was visited as regularly as possible by a circuit preacher. He appointed a class leader, a lay person, who presided over a weekly meeting of the membership. Prayer, study, admonition, and mutual encouragement forged a bond which, between the preacher's sometimes infrequent visits, kept the faithful together and growing. The class-meeting system was extensively and effectively employed in the Evangelical Association and the United Brethren Church, as well as in Methodism.

Each of the churches also had developed a structure with established patterns of authority and responsibility, thus making it possible to monitor progress, marshal resources, and map strategy. For example, general and annual conferences had been created to legislate policy, and bishops were elected to implement the legislation.

Language Restrictions

A third growth factor was expansion into work among English-speaking people by the Evangelicals and the United

Brethren. The ministry of each of these churches before 1816 was confined almost exclusively to the German-speaking population. Then it became evident to many of their leaders that they could effectively enlarge their ministry by reaching out to those who spoke English. Furthermore, many suspected that the use of the German language might decline as generations passed. After considerable debate and deliberation, work among the English-speaking began. John McNamar, licensed in 1813, was the first English-language preacher among the United Brethren. Others were licensed shortly thereafter.

Between 1820 and 1850, there was much agitation within the Evangelical Association to expand its ministry to the English-speaking; and by 1830 there were several English-language preachers in the church. Fearful that the German-language base of the church would be eroded, however, the General Conference of 1830 held that only preachers with some knowledge of German were acceptable for licensing. This restriction may have hampered the general growth of the Evangelical Association until 1843, when the General Conference decided to give more attention to work among English-speaking people. Ironically, Methodism, in which ministry was almost solely to the English-speaking, began work among the German-speaking in the 1830s.

Worship, Education, Mission, Publication

Many of the most important developments in the churches during the 1816–1843 period involved four areas: worship, education and the Sunday school, mission, and publication. Each of these deserves some attention.

Worship

Worship was of central importance. Scripture reading, preaching, exhorting, praying, and singing were prominent when the people gathered in homes, church buildings, and camp meetings. Hymn singing was very popular. Hymns were often

73

taught by the preacher or song leader, who "lined" them for the congregation until a hymn became familiar. Affordable and portable hymnbooks were also available. Among the more popular hymns were "O, For a Thousand Tongues to Sing"; "Love Divine, All Loves Excelling"; and "Come, Thou Fount of Every Blessing." But the focal point of worship was the sermon, based upon a passage of scripture and usually preached with verve and conviction. It was commonplace for the sermon or service to end with a call for repentance, acceptance of Christ, and an invitation to join the church.

Both adult and infant baptism were practiced in all three churches, and suitable baptismal rituals were provided in their books of discipline. The mode of baptism varied widely; immersion, pouring, and sprinkling were employed. The Lord's Supper was highly esteemed, though it was celebrated infrequently. Methodists, for example, generally held quarterly observances of the Lord's Supper, perhaps because of the scarcity of clergy to administer it. Each church prescribed a ritual by which it was to be celebrated, but some ministers preferred to follow their own forms. Among all three churches the use of wine was common, although dissent appeared because of the influence of the temperance movement.

Other worship practices continued among the Methodists. Love feasts were powerful occasions for the sharing of personal spiritual testimonies and the passing from hand to hand of bread and water, symbolic of an intimate family meal. Watch nights were occasional services of praise, thanksgiving, and the renewal of one's covenant with God, held especially on the New Year. Prayer meetings were scheduled weekly and congregational fasts now and then. The United Brethren occasionally held footwashing services.

The churches became more active in the construction of meeting places, although classes continued to meet in private homes, and camp-meeting grounds provided an earthy setting for revivals. The earliest meetinghouses were simple structures. Some were nothing more than large log cabins or frame buildings, especially on the frontier. In the more settled regions, buildings were often erected following the Federal style of architecture. The dress of the clergy was usually pain and simple, but some Methodist preachers preferred to wear gowns.

Education

Education was another area of the churches' interest. All three churches promoted Sunday schools. The preachers of the Methodist Episcopal Church were ordered "to encourage the establishment and progress of Sunday schools" by the General Conference of 1824. Three years later, the Methodist Sunday School Union was founded to promote the expansion of Sunday schools and to consolidate their strength as an integral part of the Methodist Episcopal Church. Its publishing house was directed to supply acceptable literature for the Sunday schools.

It is believed that the first Sunday school of the Evangelical Association was organized in Lebanon, Pennsylvania, in 1832. The General Conference of 1835 resolved that "German Sabbath Schools" were to be established wherever possible, and gradually, the Sunday school movement grew in the Evangelical Association. It is more difficult to determine when the United Brethren began their Sunday school work; it may have been as early as 1820. The church encouraged the expansion of Sunday schools and provided materials for them through its publishing house.

Educational institutions were also on the churches' agenda during this era. Methodists instituted preparatory schools, such as Wesleyan Academy in 1815, at Wilbraham, Massachusetts, and a number of colleges. Among the latter were Randolph-Macon College in Virginia (1830), Wesleyan University in Connecticut (1831), and McKendree College in Illinois (1835). Both the United Brethren and the Evangelical Association discussed the matter of educational institutions, and the United Brethren opened the first of several colleges, Otterbein University, in Westerville, Ohio, in 1847. The Evangelical Association delayed the launching of a school until 1852, when it started Albright Seminary at Berlin, Pennsylvania.

By the third and fourth decades of the nineteenth century, the churches that now compose The United Methodist Church were sufficiently confident of their human talents and material resources to begin developing colleges, orphanages, mission boards, publishing houses, and agencies of moral reform, in response to their understanding of Jesus' teachings.

There was ample disagreement in the churches concerning the education of their ministers. Numerous reasons were offered in opposition to any formal theological education for preachers; the call of God to the ministry was regarded as the only necessary preparation. Theological education would probably lessen the preacher's zeal for evangelism and personal piety. It might expose young preachers to unorthodox views. It would cause divisiveness in the ministry between those who had been educated and those who had not. It took time from saving souls and threatened to create an intellectual gap between the clergy and laity.

In spite of the opposition, however, there was some sentiment to institute an educational program that would ensure a more knowledgeable ministry. The 1816 General Conference of the Methodist Episcopal Church recommended that the annual conferences organize "a course of reading and study proper to be pursued by candidates for the ministry," but the proposal was not uniformly implemented. Some annual conferences developed effective study programs, while others were lax. The 1843 General Conference of the Evangelical Association and the United Brethren General Conference of 1845 enacted legislation that established courses of study for their preachers. Theological seminaries generally were held in great disdain by all three churches, although a few voices advocated formal theological training. Methodists in New England, for example, succeeded in founding an institution for theological instruction. It opened in 1841 as the Newbury Biblical Institute in Newbury, Vermont.

Mission

Mission work represents the third principal activity of the period. The churches were interested in reaching the unconverted both at home and abroad. Among the earliest Methodist missionaries was John Stewart, a man of mixed ancestry, who worked among the Wyandot Indians of Ohio about 1816. Missionary societies were organized to develop strategies and provide funds for this work. In 1838 the German Evangelical

Missionary Society of North America was begun under the sponsorship of the eastern conference of the Evangelical Association. Its purpose was "to make arrangements and provide means, to extend and promote the kingdom of God, by missionaries." One year later, in the belief that the whole church would participate in a formal mission program, the General Missionary Society of the Evangelical Association was formed. Women's auxiliaries of the General Society were organized in the same year. Mission work extended the ministry in the western as well as the eastern sections of the church.

The Parent Missionary Society of the United Brethren in Christ was established by the 1841 General Conference. Conferences, circuits, and local churches were urged to organize mission societies and seek funds for mission work. The United Brethren extended their missionary efforts into northern New York, Canada, and the West.

The Missionary Society of the Methodist Episcopal Church was established in 1820 by the General Conference. The successor to earlier unofficial missionary organizations, its purpose was to raise funds for mission work and keep the importance of missionary endeavor before the attention of the church. Missions on the frontier and in the cities, among Native Americans and African Americans, were undertaken by various annual conferences and by the Missionary Society. The denomination's first "foreign" missionary projects included those in Liberia (1833) and South America (1835).

Publication

Publication was a fourth area of involvement. John Wesley had set an important example for Methodism by his own reading and study habits. He was convinced that Christians could mature by reading Christian literature, so he encouraged the printing and distribution of what he considered edifying material. American Methodism followed his lead. The Methodist Book Concern, founded in 1789, was the first denominational publishing house in America. It continued to make available to Methodists and to others a selection of carefully chosen books and tracts, many of which were from the pen of John Wesley. In the nineteenth century, under the supervision of capable managers such as Joshua Soule, Nathan Bangs, and Beverly Waugh, the Book Concern not only offered an impressive list of books and pamphlets, but succeeded in printing a theological journal for the denomination. It also published materials for women, children, youth, and the Sunday school. In 1826 it began publication of a weekly newspaper titled the *Christian Advocate*, which was important for keeping the general membership informed. The printing operations and management of the Book Concern, originally in Philadelphia, were moved to New York City in 1804. A branch was subsequently opened in Cincinnati, and by mid-century a number of "depositories" were established in other cities. Book Concern profits were designated for the support of retired preachers and the widows and orphans of preachers.

The Evangelical Association contracted with private printers to publish materials as early as 1809. By 1816 the church had purchased printing equipment and property to establish its own press in New Berlin, Pennsylvania. German-language hymnals, books of discipline, and other religious literature were produced for the membership. But not until 1832 did the church authorize an English book of discipline and hymnbook. A newspaper, *Christian Messenger*, for the general membership, began publication in 1836.

The United Brethren also worked with private printing businesses to produce materials, mostly hymnals and books of discipline, until the General Conference of 1833 authorized a Printing Establishment. This was located at Circleville, Ohio, and an official denominational newspaper, the *Religious Telescope*, was begun in 1834. Profits from the printing operations were designated for retired and "indigent" preachers and their families.

Democratic Crises and the Methodist Protestant Church

A number of church crises reflected the democratic mood that carried Andrew Jackson to the White House in 1828. For example, there was a dispute in the United Brethren Church between 1837 and 1841 concerning the role of the laity in amending the church's constitution.

Methodism was ruptured by the founding of the Methodist Protestant Church in 1830. During the first three decades of the nineteenth century, a strong concern arose in Methodism for broader participation by preachers and people in the life of the church. A "reform" party which surfaced in the 1820s advocated three causes: (1) the election of district superintendents rather than their appointment by the bishops; (2) full conference membership for local preachers; and (3) most important of all, representation of the laity with the clergy in the policymaking conferences of the church. As a result of their agitation, some preachers and laypeople involved in the reform movement were either suspended or expelled from the church in 1827. Later that year, they held a convention in Baltimore, the storm center of the dissent. The reformers pressed their cause again at the General Conference of 1828, but lost. Nevertheless, the movement continued to grow, and its leaders met again in Baltimore in November 1830 to organize the Methodist Protestant Church, with an initial membership of five thousand. The new church's constitution eliminated the offices of bishop and district superintendent, secured lay representation from each circuit and station in annual conferences, and equal ministerial and lay representation at the General Conference, over which a president would preside. Local preachers, however, did not gain annual conference membership.

Chapter Five

Slavery, Division, and Civil War

1843 to 1865

Shortly after the American Revolution, the number of voices raised against slavery increased. More Americans recognized the contradiction between the liberty for which the colonists had fought and the practice of slavery. Some, soon called abolitionists, argued that the dream of America as a Christian nation could never be realized as long as slavery existed among its people. Abolitionist sentiment grew slowly, often supported by the Second Great Awakening's concern for social reform, but not without strong misgivings and vigorous opposition.

Until about 1830, a philosophy of gradual emancipation prevailed. But when William Lloyd Garrison founded the American Anti-Slavery Society in 1833 and demanded immediate freedom for slaves, radical polarization of the nation began. Although the abolitionist movement incurred opposition in both North and South, it became apparent by 1840 that slavery was evolving into a sectional issue that could threaten the nation's solidarity, as well as the unity of those Protestant churches with substantial memberships in both sections of the country. For example, the slavery question was a key factor in dividing Presbyterians and Baptists into northern and southern factions.

While the Evangelical Association and the United Brethren Church experienced some of the tensions created by the slavery problem, they did not suffer widespread divisiveness. Yet the fact that between 1841 and 1845, the United Brethren closed the pages of their denominational paper to the slavery controversy for fear its circulation would be impaired, indicates that their church was not entirely insulated from the dispute. Nevertheless, both denominations adopted a strong position against slavery. The 1816 General Conference of the Evangelical Association counseled its members to avoid the "buying and selling of men and women, whereby slavery is introduced or promoted." Their General Conference of 1839 prohibited the membership from owning or trading slaves. The third General Conference of the United Brethren, held in 1821, adopted the following legislation:

> Resolved and enacted, that no slavery, in whatever form it may exist, and in no sense of the word, shall be permitted or tolerated in our church; and should there be found any persons holding slaves, who are members among us, or make application to become such, then the former cannot remain, and the latter cannot become members of the United Brethren in Christ, unless they manumit their slaves as soon as they receive directions from the annual conference so to do. Neither shall any member of our church have the right to sell any of the slaves which he or she may now hold.

Methodists and Abolition

The Methodist Protestant Church and the Methodist Episcopal Church felt the full impact of the abolitionist quarrel; neither could avoid a formal sectional split after years of dispute. Since the Methodist Episcopal Church was a large and influential religious body in both North and South, it is probable that its division contributed to heightening the political disunity which finally divided the nation in 1861.

Methodism lived in the shadow of John Wesley's hatred of slavery. He had condemned it in his tract *Thoughts Upon Slavery*, published in 1774. He viewed slavery as "the sum of all villainies" and American slavery as "the vilest under the sun."

The slavery issue brewed in the Methodist Episcopal Church for several decades before it resulted in schism. Although antislavery agitation intensified at the 1836 and 1840 General Conferences, the church managed to avoid a breach. Many Methodists in both North and South supported slavery for religious and biblical reasons, as well as out of economic expediency. Some held that the question was purely political, unrelated to religion, and implored the church to remain aloof. The bishops feared that the issue would split the church, and in 1836, they said that they had "come to the solemn conviction that the only safe, scriptural and prudent way for us, both as ministers and people, to take, is wholly to refrain from the agitating subject."

Antislavery strength was gathering, however, particularly in the northern and western sections of the church. Orange Scott, a prominent ministerial member of the New England Conference and a vehement opponent of slavery, urged those with antislavery leanings to separate themselves from the Methodist Episcopal Church because it would not officially condemn the enslavement of human beings, and in 1843 he organized the Wesleyan Methodist Church. His views probably accelerated antislavery activity among northern Methodists. The stage was set for decisive consideration of the problem.

The General Conference of 1844

The Methodist Episcopal General Conference of 1844 met in New York City. It was the longest ever held and recorded the largest number of roll-call votes of any such meeting. It struggled with two fundamental and interrelated issues: slavery, and the relationship between the power of the General Conference and that of the bishops.

Two cases concerning slavery were presented to the delegates. The first involved an appeal by Francis Harding, a member of the Baltimore Annual Conference, who had been suspended for failing to free slaves acquired in marriage. The General Conference denied his appeal for reinstatement, a clear victory for the antislavery forces.

The second case involved Bishop James O. Andrew, one of the church's five episcopal leaders. Bishop Andrew had acquired two slaves, property of his first wife, who had bequeathed them to him upon her death. Furthermore, his second wife also owned slaves, although they remained her property and under her control. Andrew, therefore, rightly claimed that he had never bought or sold a slave. He stated that circumstances did not permit the emancipation of his family's slaves. Following lengthy debate, the General Conference approved a compromise resolution which required Andrew to suspend the exercise of his episcopal duties as long as the slavery "impediment" remained. A minority report protested the action against Andrew, and soon a reply criticizing the protest was drafted and adopted.

Within a few days, a Plan of Separation was presented to the delegates: It allowed the annual conferences in slaveholding states to form their own distinct church, if they desired; local churches and conferences in the border states were free to choose, by majority vote, how they would align themselves if a new church were constituted; clergy were given free choice in selecting which church they would join. There were also provisions concerning the distribution of property, especially that of the Book Concern.

While the slavery question appeared to be paramount at the 1844 General Conference, another debate revolved around differing positions on church governance. The "conference" party, supported by a majority of the delegates, argued for a unilateral focus of power in the General Conference. It held that the bishops were only officers of the General Conference, from which they derived whatever authority they possessed. The General Conference could discipline, as in the case of Bishop Andrew, and even expel, any bishop who was guilty of violating its dictates. The opposition, identified as the "constitutional" party, held that the constitution of the church placed the focus of power coordinately in the General Conference and the episcopacy, and that therefore the disciplinary action against Bishop Andrew was unconstitutional.

Formation of the Methodist Episcopal Church, South

Within a year after the adoption of the Plan of Separation by the 1844 General Conference, delegates from annual conferences in the slaveholding states met in Louisville, Kentucky.

They resolved to separate from the Methodist Episcopal Church and create a new body called the Methodist Episcopal Church, South; at the same time, a desire was expressed to maintain fraternal relations with the Methodist Episcopal Church. Separate arrangements were made for publishing, educational, and missionary work. Bishops James O. Andrew and Joshua Soule were invited to be the episcopal leaders of the new body. The first General Conference of the new church was convened in Petersburg, Virginia, in 1846, and a book of discipline and a hymnbook were authorized at that meeting.

Among the members of the Methodist Episcopal Church, reactions to the separation were mixed. While some found nothing objectionable about the course of events begun at the General Conference in 1844, others questioned the expediency and constitutionality of the Plan of Separation. In addition, there were numerous conflicts concerning the status of churches and annual conferences on the boundary between the two major sections of Methodism; rivalry was intense between the two churches for the loyalty of Methodists living in those states.

The 1848 General Conference of the northern church revealed hostility to the separation. Fewer than a third of the delegates to the 1844 General Conference were reelected. The 1848 meeting adopted a resolution not to enter into fraternal relations with the southern church and declared the Plan of Separation unconstitutional. Although the northern church could not force a reunion, since division was an accomplished fact, it could avenge the illegal breach by trying to withhold from the southern church an equitable distribution of the assets of the Book Concern. After lengthy litigation, however, the Federal courts awarded the southern church a share of the assets. The 1854 General Conference of the southern church selected Nashville, Tennessee, as the location of its publishing house.

Northern and Southern Methodists Go Their Own Way

The bitterness between the northern and southern churches continued into and beyond the 1850s. Each held general

85

conferences, and each considered a variety of issues, some of which would change the life of Methodism long after the slavery question was put to rest. For example, the 1852 General Conference of the northern church considered petitions that recommended lay representation in the annual and general conferences, but retained by a vote of 171 to 3 the policy of no official voice for the laity.

Both churches discussed theological education. They endorsed the notion of an educated ministry, although theological education was still a subject that stirred disagreement. There was much vocal opposition in the northern church, for example, when a Methodist Episcopal seminary was proposed for New York City. The belief persisted in some quarters that a formally educated ministry would be spiritually bankrupt and would produce a chasm between the clergy and the laity. Had they so easily forgotten that John Wesley's life testified to the unity of education and spirituality?

Slavery remained a major problem in both churches during the late 1850s. The northern church was besieged by petitioners who requested the church to exclude slaveholders from its membership. Others felt that exclusion was too radical. Nevertheless, abolitionist strength continued to swell among the Methodist Episcopal members. In the southern church, the controversial provision of the General Rules which prohibited buying and selling slaves was removed in 1858. The southern church also adopted a philosophy affirming that it was not the business of the church to be involved in matters that belonged to the jurisdiction of civil institutions. Slavery was a political issue, not a moral question; therefore it was better left in the hands of the government.

Lincoln's Election and Civil War

Abraham Lincoln was elected to the presidency of the United States in 1860. By the time of his inauguration in March 1861, the southern states had begun to secede to form a new government,

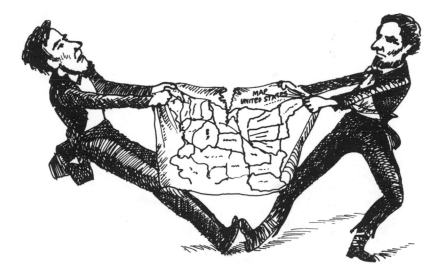

Less than a century after Americans adopted the slogan Join or Die, an attempt was made to disjoin the United States. A political cartoon of the Civil-War era shows President Abraham Lincoln and Confederate President Jefferson Davis tearing the nation's map. Nearly twenty years earlier, the Methodist Episcopal Church had been torn apart by the same questions: slavery and divergent views of government.

87

the Confederate States of America. Civil War began on April 12, 1861, when Confederates fired on Fort Sumter in the harbor of Charleston, South Carolina, and the hostilities were to continue until Lee's surrender in 1865.

The northern and southern Methodist churches, which had become the largest and wealthiest Protestant bodies in their respective geographical areas, could not remain detached from the conflict. Tensions in the border conferences intensified. The bishops, religious press, and annual conferences of the northern church faithfully supported the Union cause. They engaged in patriotic demonstrations and recruited more than five hundred chaplains for the Union Army. Valuable assistance was contributed to the United States Christian Commission, organized in 1861 to perform religious work among the troops. Methodist Episcopal clergy assisted with the enlistment of recruits. They even followed the advancing Union Army into the South, where they organized northern-type Methodist churches, an action that bred a bitterness among southern Methodists which lasted for decades.

The southern church supported the Confederacy in a like manner. It authorized chaplains, distributed Bibles and religious literature, and conducted revivals among the troops. The clergy and religious press interpreted the war to countless southerners, and most of them were as convinced as were those in the northern church that, in the fiery ordeal in which they were engaged, God's blessing rested on their side.

Chapter Six

New Challenges

1865 to 1913

When the Civil War ended in 1865, the American people confronted a multitude of questions concerning the future of the nation. How would the former Confederate states be reintegrated into the Union? Could sectional antagonism be ameliorated? What would be the status of the four million freed slaves? How could the severely war-weakened southern economy be rehabilitated? These and other acute problems were dealt with in the program of Reconstruction. Next to the war itself, Reconstruction has often been judged the most unpleasant chapter in nineteenth-century American life. Lasting into the late 1870s, it was a period filled with revenge, animosity, deceit, and misunderstanding.

The Nation Begins to Change

Probably very few Americans in 1866 could foresee the difficulties of Reconstruction or the vast changes that would occur in their nation's life during the next half-century. Industrialization of the economy, led by the pronounced growth of heavy industry and the extension of the network of railroads, continued at an ever increasing rate. Financial panics in 1873, 1893, and 1907 temporarily slowed economic growth and raised questions about the nation's economic philosophy. The expansion of industry gave birth to labor unrest and resulted in the organization of a powerful union movement. The population more than tripled its 1860 figure of 31 million; by 1915 it numbered more than 100 million.

Approximately 20 million immigrants entered the country

during this period, and the size and number of cities indicated that the nation was becoming urbanized. These centers of population yielded their social and cultural blessings as well as the blight of poverty, exploitation, and corruption. The nation was influenced by intellectual developments: Darwin's theory of evolution; the Chautauqua movement, which originated at Chautauqua, New York, as a program to promote adult education for religious and cultural purposes; the strengthening of public and private educational institutions. And American churches were involved in the changes wrought by Reconstruction and the new challenges presented by the succeeding decades.

One of the major concerns during Reconstruction was the rebuilding of the Methodist Episcopal Church, South, which had suffered with the rest of the Confederacy. The membership had fallen from 750,000 to fewer than 500,000, and its clergy ranks were depleted. Many of the southern churches had been destroyed or seriously damaged; many had lost their leadership. Publishing, educational, and mission activities had been suspended, and there were serious questions about their restoration.

Some southern Methodists favored reunion with the northern church. But it was not to be. The Palmyra Manifesto of 1865, emanating from the Missouri Annual Conference, called for the continuation of the Methodist Episcopal Church, South. Furthermore, later in 1865, the southern bishops issued a Pastoral Address declaring loyalty to their church and calling for a General Conference in 1866. That meeting established the groundwork for rebuilding the publishing, educational, and mission programs, and by 1870, it was clear that the southern church was recovering much of its prewar vitality.

Since the African American membership of the southern church had been rapidly eroding, the 1870 General Conference of the Methodist Episcopal Church, South, acted to form the Colored Methodist Episcopal Church, to which it intended to transfer all its remaining black members. A large number of its former black members had already been siphoned off by African Methodist Episcopal and African Methodist Episcopal Zion congregations organized in the south, and the Colored Methodist Episcopal Church was formally born in December 1870. William H. Miles and Richard H. Vanderhorst were elected its bishops and duly consecrated by bishops of the Methodist Episcopal Church, South. The denomination is known today as the Christian Methodist Episcopal Church.

The Churches Prosper

In spite of the difficulties of Reconstruction, the postwar decades were prosperous for the churches that currently compose The United Methodist Church. There were significant increases in membership: From 1860 through 1920, the Methodist Church, South, grew from 750,000 to more than two million; the Methodist Episcopal Church increased from one million to well over four million; membership in the Methodist Protestant Church grew from 60,000 to 185,000; the Evangelical Association, from 40,000 to 240,000; and the United Brethren in Christ, from 95,000 to 350,000. The number of congregations increased and the churches became more affluent. Between the Civil War and World War I, the churches rejoiced in their progress and endured the stresses that characterized the period.

Publishing, Education, Worship

Still convinced that the printed page was a useful means for evangelizing, nurturing, and informing, the churches maintained their strong publishing programs. The publishing houses of the Evangelical Association and the United Brethren Church produced abundant materials for the Sunday schools, families, and clergy. Their presses printed a number of historical and theological works in addition to German- and English-language periodicals for the general membership. Financial difficulties, at times quite ominous, did not slow the three Methodist bodies from producing a steady stream of books, periodicals, and Sunday school literature. Their denominational newspapers and magazines helped to develop a solidarity among the members.

Building on their earlier involvement in Sunday schools and institutions of secondary and higher education, the churches succeeded in enlarging their instructional ministries. All of them founded additional colleges and universities, and they also sought to establish and implement higher educational standards for their clergy. Courses of study, the commonly accepted route of entry into the ministry, were made uniform across the churches and were regularly reexamined and improved. The need for a more thoroughly trained and formally educated ministry was increasingly acknowledged, and by 1900, all the churches had opened at least one graduate theological school for the professional education of their clergy. These seminaries were to play an increasingly critical role in the life of each church.

The Freedman's Aid Society deserves special mention as an important educational ministry developed after the Civil War. It was an agency of the Methodist Episcopal Church, sanctioned by the General Conference of 1868, with the primary purpose of establishing and maintaining educational institutions for freed slaves in the southern states. Among the schools started were Rust College at Holly Springs, Mississippi (1866); Clark College in Atlanta, Georgia (1869); Claflin College in Orangeburg, South Carolina (1869); and Meharry Medical College in Nashville, Tennessee (1876).

The post-Civil War period witnessed more formalized orders of worship in the churches. Elaborate organs, robed choirs, cushioned pews, and stained-glass windows helped to provide the setting. Hundreds of churches were built each year, many in the Gothic revival and Romanesque architectural styles. Preachers could be identified by black suits, which were becoming standard clergy dress. Some preferred a Prince Albert coat, white vest, and white bow tie to conduct worship. Near the turn of the century, some preachers wore a frock coat, winged collar, and striped trousers in the pulpit. Hymns, prayers, responsive readings from scripture, and preaching remained the major components of worship, set within a more orderly liturgical structure than was generally the case earlier in the nineteenth century. Some clergy and laity felt that the newer formal worship did not permit as much freedom and spontaneity as they preferred, but others praised the solemnity and beauty of the more orderly arrangements.

Popular hymns of the period included Methodist Fanny J. Crosby's "Blessed Assurance, Jesus Is Mine" and "Alas! And Did My Savior Bleed," as well as Ira Sankey's "There Were Ninety and Nine," and the African American spirituals "There Is a Balm in Gilead" and "Go, Tell It on the Mountain."

The Methodist hymnal, jointly published in 1905 by the northern and southern churches, included a dignified order of service, tasteful music, and a psalter in the form of responsive readings. Preaching, however, continued to be worship's fundamental feature, and fresh, powerful sermons were highly regarded. Revised rituals for baptism and communion were provided and more wisely used.

Theological and Structural Controversies

The era between the wars was marked by several theological and structural disagreements in the churches, some sufficiently grave to lead to schisms. One of the most disruptive debates involved the Wesleyan doctrine of holiness and sanctification. John Wesley had accentuated the importance of holy living for Christians by stressing Christian perfection. Many Methodists interpreted Christian perfection in terms of a Christian's gradual maturing in God's grace and power; others saw it as an instantaneous gift from God, a "second blessing," the "first blessing" being the sinner's conversion. American Methodism became polarized on this issue between 1870 and 1900.

A number of Methodists who favored the sudden "second blessing" approach, and found precedent for it in Wesley's theology, were instrumental in organizing a "holiness" movement among American Protestants. By means of their periodicals, camp meetings, and organizations, the "holiness people" excited reaction and encountered strenuous opposition within Methodism. Late in the nineteenth century, convinced that Methodism could not be moved to correct its lack of holiness zeal, many of the proponents of the holiness position broke from the church and participated in the formation of a group of new churches, such as the Church of the Nazarene and Pilgrim Holiness Church. The Evangelical Association also bore the pain of discord on the matter of holiness and sanctification from 1848 through 1875, though the issue was settled without a major schism.

Other theological and structural questions troubled the churches. The United Brethren in Christ (Old Constitution) was formed by members of the United Brethren who objected to theological and constitutional legislation adopted at their General Conference of 1889. Discord among Evangelicals over the power of bishops, and a keen rivalry among the denomination's leaders, led to a schism in 1894, when the United Evangelical Church was founded.

The rise of theological liberalism was also a source of quarrels in the churches. Darwin's theory of evolution was a central issue in these arguments, as was the scientific method of understanding the Bible, which called into question old conclusions as to the authorship, chronology, and accuracy of the text of scripture. The liberal stress on the immanence and love of God, rather than God's transcendence and judgment, was debated. There was also much contention over the liberal emphasis on the humanness of Jesus, to the exclusion of his divinity.

Lay Participation

Long before the Civil War, the laity had asked for a greater voice in determining the policies and actions of the churches. The Methodist Protestant Church had granted lay people official representation in its annual conferences and General Conference at the time of its formation in 1830. It was not until after the war, however, and not without decades of debate, that the Methodist Episcopal Church, the Methodist Episcopal Church, South, the United Brethren, and the Evangelical Association granted the laity an official voice at regional and national levels. The clergy were reluctant to concede the point, but by 1932, lay people had become voting delegates in the annual and general conferences of all the churches, and ultimately they were granted representation equal to that of the clergy. Lay membership in the conferences and in the growing host of church boards and agencies opened new opportunities at the national and regional levels for lay people to exercise the leadership they displayed in business and in their local congregations.

Women continued to occupy important roles in local churches, though usually unheralded for their work in the Sunday schools, missionary organizations, and other important areas of congregational life. Among Methodists, for example, Ladies' Aid Societies in local churches furnished the parsonages and sponsored social events. In 1911 the Methodist Book Concern published *The Ladies' Aid Manual,* which described how these groups should be organized and suggested activities that would "contribute to the social, intellectual, and financial development of the church without incurring any just criticism."

A struggle to involve women in the broader life of the churches was waged on at least two fronts. First, women were ineligible for lay offices in the church or for the newly won lay representation in the conferences. When the 1888 General Conference of the Methodist Episcopal Church was held in New York City, five prominent women, including Frances E. Willard, the famous leader of the Woman's Christian Temperance Union, were properly elected as delegates. Since women had never before been elected or seated as regular delegates at a General Conference, the question of their eligibility was raised. After spirited debate, the conference decided that "laymen" meant *men* and refused to seat the women for constitutional, sociological, and theological reasons. The right of women to be regular delegates to a General Conference of the Methodist Episcopal Church was not finally resolved until 1904, when women were elected and admitted without question.

The second area of contention regarding the role of women concerned the question of their licensing and ordination as preachers. Women could serve the church as missionaries and deaconesses, but could they be licensed to preach and be ordained? No women were ordained in the Evangelical Association; and although women had applied for licenses to preach among the United Brethren early in the 1840s, the first woman to obtain permission was Charity Opheral, in 1847. Four years later, Lydia Sexton was regarded as "a Christian lady of useful gifts as a pulpit speaker" and was recommended as "a useful helper in the work of Christ." Not until 1889 did the United Brethren General Conference approve the ordination of women, but by 1901, nearly a hundred women were listed in its ministerial directory.

The New York Conference of the Methodist Protestant Church ordained Anna Howard Shaw in 1880. Her ordination caused dissension within the denomination and was declared unlawful, but her annual conference recognized her orders. Ordination for women in both northern and southern Methodist Episcopal churches was resisted. A major test case was brought before the northern Methodist Episcopal General Conference in 1880, and not only did that General Conference deny women the right of ordination, it also refused to license women as local preachers! Women were not granted full clergy rights in either church until after reunion in 1939.

Missionary Work

The five decades preceding the outbreak of World War I witnessed an explosive growth of Protestant missionary efforts. There was a renewed urgency to evangelize the unconverted people of the earth and to recruit them for church membership.

96

One or two women were recognized as potential preachers by the United Brethren in the 1840s, but women were not approved for ordination by that denomination until 1889. A Methodist Protestant woman was ordained in 1880, but the Evangelical, Methodist Episcopal, and Methodist Episcopal, South, churches never did grant women full clergy rights during that time.

97

This fervor was two-dimensional, in that it emphasized home missions, including work among the unchurched in the cities, farmlands, and frontier, and it also included foreign or overseas missions.

The churches supported and improved their missionary agencies. The Evangelical Association and the United Brethren had official denominational boards which promoted their work at home and in such distant locales as Africa, Germany, China, Japan, and the Philippines. Each had active women's organizations, which upheld the work with personnel, funds, and educational programs.

The northern and southern Methodists carried on effective mission work among the Native Americans, often competing keenly with each other as they expanded and strengthened their work in such territories as Colorado, Montana, Wyoming, Oregon, and California. They had begun work in China, India, and Europe before the Civil War; after that war, they enlarged their efforts in those areas and added other missions in Asia, Africa, and Latin America. The Methodist Protestant Church also sponsored home and foreign work, though before World War I, this was largely confined to Japan.

Women were leaders in the missionary movement. Through their offerings and educational and recruitment endeavors, and their own enlistment to serve on the mission field, women contributed invaluable assistance to the missionary crusade. The Woman's Foreign Missionary Society of the Methodist Episcopal Church was born in 1869. Eleven years later, those women formed the Woman's Home Missionary Society. Similar groups were formed by Methodist Episcopal Church, South, and Methodist Protestant women. The United Brethren and Evangelical Association women also had mission societies prior to 1900. Local units of all these denominational organizations were found in almost every local church shortly after they were formed.

Important home mission work centered on the needs of immigrant and ethnic groups in America. The Evangelical

Association and the United Brethren in Christ, with their predominantly German cultural and language origins, had a natural advantage in attracting the German immigrant population. The Methodists developed work among the Germans largely due to the leadership of William Nast, a well-educated German immigrant, converted in 1835. Nast was instrumental in organizing the first German Methodist society in America in 1838. Methodist home mission work also was begun among Scandinavians, Japanese, Chinese, Italians, Cubans, Mexicans, and Native Americans. Some of this activity became sufficiently substantial to be organized into ethnic annual conferences; the rest was preserved in bilingual missions. Important milestones among American Methodists were reached in 1873 when Alejo Hernandez became the first ordained Hispanic pastor, and in 1887 when Kanichi Miyama, a Japanese pastor, was granted full clergy rights.

Two important facts must be noted at this point. First, the Methodist work among the various language groups in America supplied the impetus for missions to Germany and the Scandinavian countries. Methodist churches were founded in those European nations as a result of the affiliations of many of their sons and daughters in America. Second, the ministries to immigrants were not without the tensions created by a periodically resurgent American nativism which resented the economic, political, and cultural threats posed by the new-comers. The churches sometimes found themselves strained between a commitment to assist the recently arrived in spiritual and material ways and a wish that they had stayed in their native lands. In this matter, the churches reflected the ambivalence of the larger society.

Social Problems

American Protestants responded to late nineteenth-century social problems such as alcoholism, child labor, and life in urban slums in at least two ways. Some believed that the best solution was traditional revivalism, as updated by Dwight L. Moody and other evangelists: Convert the individual, and ultimately society would be reformed. Others insisted that economic, political, and social problems were more than individual issues, and therefore society's institutions must be reformed. A movement known as Social Christianity, or the Social Gospel, emerged from the latter group. Although it was quite diverse, that movement was one of the most important Protestant ventures between the Civil War and World War I.

The churches whose histories we are investigating supported both the revivalistic and the Social Gospel crusades. And since those two philosophies of dealing with social problems were often incompatible, it is not surprising that there were conflicts in the churches between the proponents of each. Nevertheless, the churches recognized the necessity of speaking to, and acting upon, the social problems that plagued the nation.

Alcoholic beverages were identified as a major cause of social and individual decay; therefore, the churches actively promoted total abstinence. The Methodists, the Evangelical Association, and the United Brethren each had a history of opposition to alcohol going back to the period before the Civil War. After the war, they became very active in the campaign to outlaw alcoholic beverages, utilizing moral persuasion and political action to achieve the goal of total abstinence. One extraordinary national figure in the crusade against alcohol was Frances E. Willard, a member of the Methodist Episcopal Church and also an ardent proponent of women's rights.

The churches underscored their disdain for the consumption of alcoholic beverages by using grape juice in their communion services. In the Methodist Episcopal Church, for example, grape juice was recommended by the General Conference of 1864. By 1880, it was required "whenever practicable," but not until 1916 was it made mandatory without qualification.

Remembering the importance of ministering to the poor and underprivileged, the churches opened various charitable institutions, most of them in the years following the Civil War.

Methodists were especially active in this endeavor, and although they had founded a home for the elderly in New York City as early as 1850, northern Methodists established several others in the years immediately after the war. They opened their first hospital in Brooklyn in 1887. Homes for children were also organized, the first being the German Methodist Orphan Asylum in Berea, Ohio, in 1864. By 1913, all the churches now included in United Methodism had founded various charitable facilities to serve the needy.

Methodist, United Brethren, and Evangelical women also organized deaconess movements in their churches to visit, evangelize, and minister to the poor and sick in some communities in the United States and overseas. Lucy Rider Meyer, Isabella Thoburn, and Belle Harris Bennett were leaders of the deaconess movement among Methodists. The Methodist Episcopal Church established the office of deaconess in 1888; shortly, the other churches officially authorized the ministry of deaconesses, and deaconess work grew significantly over the ensuing years.

The plight of workers was another principal concern of the Social Gospel. While many church leaders and members opposed unionization and strikes, some spoke in behalf of the workers. Because the Methodist Episcopal Church and the Methodist Episcopal Church, South, were often controlled by the middle class, they sometimes appeared indifferent to the conditions of the laboring class. Yet the Methodist Federation for Social Service, founded in 1907, and the Social Creed, legislated by the 1908 General Conference, prove that the northern church was not oblivious to the situation of the worker. The creed called for "equal rights and complete justice for all men in all stations of life." It favored labor unions, improvement of working conditions, a living and equitable wage, and protection for women and children in the work force. The Methodist Social Creed served as a pattern for the social concerns document of the Federal Council of Churches.

The plight of workers concerned many Christians during the closing years of the nineteenth century, although they were divided in their attitudes toward unions and strikes. By 1908, however, the Methodist Episcopal Church was ready to favor unions, improvement of working conditions, equitable wages, and protection for women and children in the work force.

NEW CHALLENGES (1865–1913)

Interchurch Cooperation

Despite occasional schismatic developments in the late nineteenth and early twentieth centuries, there were important developments in interchurch cooperation, and even negotiations for union. The United Brethren were involved in conversations with the Methodist Protestant and Congregational churches for several years after the turn of the century. The Evangelical Association and the Methodist Episcopal Church discussed union between 1859 and 1871; when negotiations failed to materialize, the Evangelical Association strengthened its ties and fellowship with the United Brethren.

Efforts were made to improve the relationship between the Methodist Episcopal Church and the Methodist Episcopal Church, South. Delegations from both churches met in Cape May, New Jersey, in 1876 to discuss their mutual ties and to affirm a sense of fraternity; although reunion would not occur for more than sixty years, the groundwork was laid for the conversations and actions that would bring it to pass.

The Ecumenical Methodist Conferences held in 1881, 1891, 1901, and 1911 were another means by which churches of the worldwide Methodist family gathered to discuss their home and foreign work, promote cooperation, and increase their common moral and evangelical power.

Not only did the spirit of cooperation flourish among the five forerunners of United Methodism, but these churches also became parties to the larger ecumenical movement which began to flower during the decades preceding World War I. Each of them joined the Federal Council of Churches, the first major ecumenical venture among American Protestants. Its purposes were to "express the fellowship and catholic unity of the Christian Church" and to "secure a larger combined influence for the churches of Christ in all matters affecting the moral and social condition of the people, so as to promote the application of the law of Christ in every relation of human life."

103

Optimism Chokes on Reality

Nearly a century after the deaths of Albright, Boehm, Otterbein, and Asbury, the churches they started were rejoicing in their growth and basking in a feeling of optimism about the future. This sense of confidence was compounded of the Christian doctrine that God works in all things for good, and the secular doctrine that things are getting better and better all the time. But soon the secular doctrine of progress suffocated in the gas-filled trenches of World War I, and the churches found their trust in God's providence challenged by the wars, economic crises, racism, new moralities, sexism, and theological changes of the twentieth century.

Part Three

The Twentieth Century

Kenneth E. Rowe

Twentieth-century worship in the churches of United Methodism reappropriated the ancient tradition of ordered Christian worship—a tradition native to United Methodists through their Anglican, Lutheran, and Reformed roots, but a heritage largely neglected in the nineteenth century. Churches are now designed to be symbolic as well as functional, the Christian year has been rediscovered, candles join the cross on communion tables, robed choirs process down center aisles, and pastors appear in colored vestments.

Chapter Seven

Maturity and Status in the New Century

1913 to 1939

The shock of World War I brought the nineteenth century to an irrevocable close. A new world, distressed by war, depression, and what appeared to be moral chaos, emerged in its aftermath. But it was also a world of promise, blessed with lightbulbs and indoor plumbing, telephones and movies, radios and refrigerators, automobiles for new-style circuit riders, and that pearl of great price for the churches, the mimeograph machine.

At last, maturity and status were marks of the three families of churches. Small rural churches, large ones on a thousand main streets, and great cathedral-style buildings in the cities comfortably housed the people called Evangelicals, United Brethren, and Methodists on Sunday mornings. Dominantly middle class, the three churches also included the very poor and the very privileged. They were led by an increasing corps of seminary-trained pastors and able bishops, and were challenged by ambitious programs set forth by a growing number of churchwide boards and agencies. Optimistic about the prospects for a better age and confident that they had a large role to play in bringing it about, a half-million Evangelicals and United Brethren and five million Methodists were mobilized for mission.

Piety, Patriotism, and Prohibition

The early part of the twentieth century saw a new interest in peace. It was the height of respectability to condemn war as barbaric, and many believed that world peace through arbitration was just around the corner. Methodists, Evangelicals, and the United Brethren, at their general conferences between 1912 and 1916, supported these ideals.

America's entry into the war in 1917 ended all that for the time being. Although a few Americans continued to support pacifist ideals, the coming of war brought forth a crude mixture of idealism and crass nationalism, a holy crusade for democracy abroad and a stifling of freedom at home.

Evangelicals celebrated their founder Jacob Albright as a Revolutionary War hero and urged his latter-day flock to follow his example as a patriot. The Methodist press openly attacked Quakers and other pacifists. At some Evangelical, United Brethren, and German Methodist churches, cornerstones were painted yellow, pastors were threatened, and members were insulted as un-American. These actions must be seen in the context of the patriotic fervor in the country generally. Methodists, Evangelicals, and United Brethren were no more and no less involved in the militant enthusiasm than other churches. They were simply reflecting the predominant mood. Yet the churches did not yield completely to the national war fever. The United Brethren General Conference of 1917, noting that "a vein of pure German blood runs through our whole church from Otterbein to the present," passed a resolution requesting "our people everywhere to refrain from any unkind criticism of their German brethren in this country." A few Methodist annual conferences went on record as opposing patriotic excesses.

In the years that followed the Treaty of Versailles, revulsion against world war gave rise to a new wave of pacifism. Methodists, Evangelicals, and United Brethren adopted resolutions on peace and became active in peace societies until another world war loomed on the horizon to test their commitment.

In the first half of the twentieth century the emphasis on personal morality among Methodists, Evangelicals, and United Brethren was not relaxed. This concern found clearest

107

*America's entry into World War I in 1917 ended
the passion for peace previously exhibited by
Evangelicals, Methodists, and United Brethren.
The churches cooperated with the government in
what President Woodrow Wilson called a crusade
to make the world safe for democracy. Quakers
and other pacifists were attacked by the
Methodist press.*

expression in the churches' advocacy of total abstinence from alcoholic beverages. All three churches had been working on this front for almost a century. Temperance societies had long been recommended in all congregations and Sunday schools; Temperance Sunday, with its pledge, became an annual event; grape juice had been ordered for communion services since the 1880s; temperance literature of all kinds was penned, published, and promoted. By the declaration of several general conferences early in the twentieth century, the churches announced their intention to achieve moral reform through the agency of the state. During the period between the enactment of Prohibition in 1920 and its repeal in 1933, their primary public interest was to defend Prohibition.

The presidential election of 1928 brought the matter to political focus with the nomination of a Roman Catholic candidate. The prime reason the Methodists, Evangelicals, and United Brethren opposed Al Smith was not that he was Catholic, but that he was "wet." The battle was won in 1928, but the war was lost in 1933 when Prohibition was repealed. Although sobriety by law appears to be a thing of the past, United Methodists continue to struggle against alcoholism and its consequences.

Mutations Within the Connectional System

In the United Methodist understanding of the church, there has been a long-standing tension between the initial emphasis on small voluntary religious societies within "established" churches—Methodists within the Church of England, Evangelicals and United Brethren within Lutheran and Reformed churches—and the emphasis on being a distinctive denomination that has developed over the course of two centuries. These twin concepts of religious society and institutional church, with their respective values and concerns, have never been wholly reconciled. On the one hand, the basic premise of the small group is the principle of local initiative. It is in the local communities, and the small groups within them, that the Holy Spirit nurtures meaningful experiences, which then seek wider avenues of mission and outreach. On the other hand, United Methodists, believing themselves led by the same Spirit, have a long tradition of connectional administration by conferences, bishops, and program boards, and of developing every aspect of a full-fledged institutional church.

Throughout the nineteenth century, power in the several churches lay principally in the hands of the bishops and conferences. By the turn of the century, however, with big business and big government on the horizon, Evangelicals, United Brethren, and Methodists alike began to develop bureaucracy on a grand scale. The development had its beginnings with the formation of publishing houses and missionary societies in the nineteenth century, but it was not until the twentieth century that these publishing and mission boards, plus a whole family of new agencies, began to compete with bishops and conferences for power and influence in the church. Increasingly, it was the staffs of these boards who began to shape the policies and programs of the churches, which then were approved by the conferences and promoted by the bishops and district superintendents.

Fading Force of Ethnic Diversity/Modest Gains for Women

Although the heavy flow of immigration to America was greatly reduced in the early decades of the twentieth century, this did not mean the immediate end of foreign-language services, hymnbooks, books of discipline, and a cluster of ethnic annual conferences. One-third of the population in 1920 was still foreign-born. In that year, ten German, six Swedish, and two Norwegian-Danish annual conferences were flourishing in the Methodist Episcopal Church. Twenty years later, however, all had disappeared. The United Brethren quietly discontinued work in the German language in 1933; the use of German among Evangelicals had been given up in 1922. In every case, the time came when the younger members, impatient with the old ways, sought modernization and Americanization, and campaigned for the English language. The same thing has happened to the family of Asian Methodists on the West Coast, but much more slowly. In this period, only the Spanish-speaking Methodists preserved and strengthened their cultural identity.

Inspired by their success in gaining the right to vote in 1920, women revived their struggle for rights within their churches. Unlike the United Brethren, who, with the Methodist Protestants, led the way by granting laity and clergy rights to women in the 1880s, Methodists and Evangelicals resisted the trend. A major victory for laity rights for women had been won in the northern Methodist General Conference of 1900, but the Methodist Episcopal Church, South, moved more slowly in giving rights to women. As late as 1914, there was heated debate in the southern General Conference on the right of women to be elected to official boards in local churches or to hold other representative positions in the church. In 1918, that General Conference finally approved laity rights for women by a large majority.

Nevertheless, only half the battle had been won. Methodist women, South and North, were now full-fledged "laymen"—but could they be full-fledged clergy also? The 1920 General Conference of the Methodist Episcopal Church took the first step by granting local preacher's licenses to women. Four years later, Methodist women launched another offensive. The 1924 General Conference, sensing the indifference of the church at large toward the matter of the ordination of women, saw no need to recommend change. Yet there was one small breakthrough. Recognizing the "very evident and acute need for an effective sacramental ministry on the part of women in certain home and particularly the foreign fields," the conference approved the ordination of women as local preachers, giving them the right to administer the sacraments when no ordained man was present. Through these same years, the Evangelical Church and southern Methodists remained aloof from the whole movement.

111

THE TWENTIETH CENTURY

Loosening Ties to the Theological Tradition

There were clear signs in the 1890s that a theological shift was in the wind. "Liberal" Protestantism, a movement to modernize theology that had been developing for decades, caught up with Evangelicals and United Brethren as well as Methodists. But until 1930, the older patterns of evangelical theology inherited from the previous century were still dominant.

A bitter battle raged between conservatives and liberals (Fundamentalists and Modernists, using their own labels) in the 1920s. Conservatives saw the liberals as subversives of the faith; liberals saw themselves as saviors of the essence of the faith. By the end of the decade the conservatives had lost control and the liberals were in command, first in the seminaries and then in the church generally—on the episcopal bench, in the boards and agencies, behind the editorial desks, and in the pulpits and Sunday school classrooms across the land.

Traces of traditional evangelicalism—the centrality of Jesus Christ, the stress on personal salvation, and the longing for God's kingdom—continued, but each with a new twist. Convinced that to know the good is to do it, liberals preferred to talk about Christ as teacher, rather than as Redeemer. Confident that gradualism was the normal pattern of Christian growth, liberals abandoned the older pattern of sudden conversion. Certain that evangelical otherworldliness needed to be traded for a focus on this world, they located God's kingdom more and more in this world and thus made building the kingdom more and more a human responsibility. This led to the most crucial change of all, as far as the legacy from Wesley, Otterbein, and Albright is concerned. Liberals tended to displace the older optimism of grace, based on what God does in us through the Holy Spirit, with a new optimism of nature, based on what we do on our own apart from God.

The reigning liberal theology of the time called for changes in the rituals of all but the Evangelicals, whose form of worship had a minimum of ritual. The United Brethren revised their rituals in

1921, and the new hymnal of 1935 contained more elaborate worship resources. The southern Methodists remained the most conservative, making only minor changes in the services derived from Wesley's prayerbook. Northern Methodists were less reluctant to change: Minor changes occurred in 1916; major changes, in 1932. A new Methodist hymnal, jointly produced in 1935 by the Methodists, North and South, and the Methodist Protestants, contained four orders for Sunday worship, including a modest revision of Wesley's formal order for Morning Prayer. The trend was heavily in the direction of dignified order, in both liturgy and music. Only the African American Methodist churches retained the spontaneity, rhythmic music, and high degree of participation characteristic of nineteenth-century worship patterns.

Church architecture and worship habits reflected the times. The trend everywhere was toward more formal structures. By the 1920s the churches were in the midst of a Gothic revival. Victorian churches built on the Akron plan—semicircular sanctuaries with curved pews on sloping floors, with central pulpits and choir lofts behind—gave way to pseudo-Gothic "cathedrals," complete with divided chancels and elaborate altars. Choral music came to be a normal part of worship, often at the expense of congregational singing. The Christian year was rediscovered, along with liturgical colors; candles joined the cross on countless communion tables; robed choirs processed down center aisles, and ministers appeared in pulpit gowns instead of cutaways. The once popular midweek prayer meeting fell victim to Edgar Bergen and Charlie McCarthy, Fibber McGee and Molly, and the Lux Radio Theater.

In this period, standards of preaching also changed. Moving away from the style of the free evangelists now frowned upon, sermons were better structured and full of literary allusions, testimony to the "higher standards" set by seminary preaching courses. And these changes in worship reflected changes in the worshipers.

The Rocky Roads to Reunion:
Evangelicals in 1922; Methodists in 1939

As the Methodist, Evangelical, and United Brethren churches grew, they also divided. During the early decades of the twentieth century, however, Evangelicals and Methodists wound their way down what turned out to be rocky roads to reunion. Both churches found rocks in the way—for the Evangelicals, mostly personalities; for the Methodists, the presence of a large number of African Americans in the northern church. Both divisions were sectional in nature—East versus West for the Evangelicals; North versus South for the Methodists.

For many years rivalry simmered between two factions of the Evangelical Association. The western Indianapolis-based majority favored the German language, strong bishops, and a conservative theological stance; the eastern Philadelphia-based minority favored English, a curtailed episcopacy, and an openness to new theological developments. In 1891 there was a split that was not healed until 1922. The newly united church was christened the Evangelical Church.

Black slavery and the white racism that supported it were among the causes of Methodist divisions. By the turn of the century, great difficulties arose from the presence of both northern and southern white Methodist churches in the South; the northern branch of Methodism had begun to open churches in the South in the closing days of the Civil War. Infighting, especially bitter in the border states, caused the two churches to seek a resolution of their differences. Other influences also were at work toward the reunification of northern and southern Methodists—fraternal delegates appeared at each other's general conferences; rivalries were adjusted on the foreign mission field; both churches actively supported the work of emerging ecumenical bodies, such as the Federal Council of Churches. The two churches even began to sing and pray alike, since they produced common hymnals and rituals in 1905 and

114

again in 1935. As a result of these and other factors, Methodists, North and South, early in this century began to wind their way down the rocky road to reunion.

Throughout all those years of talking union, the one constant rock that made the road rougher was the presence of a significant number of African Americans in the northern Methodist church. In 1916, the year when union talks began in earnest, the southern church had no black members, while the northern church had more than a quarter of a million. Was it possible to devise a basis for union that would not offend southern sensibilities and yet would adhere to the North's historic mission to the African Americans?

Differing approaches to the office of bishop, the authority of the General Conference, the idea of jurisdictions, and especially the status of black ministers and members, led to the failure of a preliminary plan of union in 1924. The South talked of "absorption," the North of "regionalism." Hopes for a speedy reunion were dashed until the end of the decade, when several Methodist Protestant leaders proposed a fresh start on a three-way union. Teams of negotiators were authorized at the three churches' next general conferences. The joint commission began work at once, and by 1935 had hammered out a plan of union, the most controversial feature of which was the proposed jurisdictional structure of the new church. The country was to be divided into six administrative units—five by geography and one by race.

To be adopted, the plan of union needed to receive constitutional majorities from the general and annual confer-ences of the uniting churches. The plan's first test came at the General Conference of the Methodist Protestant Church in May 1936, where it was approved by a wide margin after modest debate. Large-scale debate occurred at the General Conference of the Methodist Episcopal Church later that month. The key issue was whether segregation was being legislated into the church. Supporters of the plan said that it was not; they argued that it was nothing more than the continuation of the policy of the

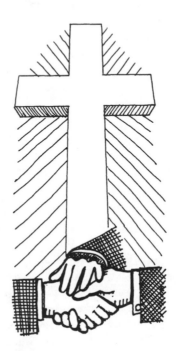

The twentieth century has witnessed a number of church reunions. Two Evangelical factions formed the Evangelical Church in 1922. Three Methodist churches—Methodist Episcopal, Methodist Protestant, and Methodist Episcopal, South—came together in The Methodist Church in 1939. The Church of the United Brethren in Christ and the Evangelical Church created the Evangelical United Brethren Church in 1946. At a uniting conference held in Dallas, Texas, in 1968, the Methodist and Evangelical United Brethren churches became The United Methodist Church.

northern church since the Civil War. Critics replied that whatever had happened in the past was past; they pointed out that although the church had been living with segregated annual conferences for almost a century, this was the moment to change the pattern, not to imbed it more deeply into the church's life and constitution. Drafters of the plan claimed that the intent behind the all-black Central Jurisdiction was not segregationist, but an arrangement to protect the African American minority in the new church, since each jurisdiction elected its own bishops and had equal representation on the general program boards of the church.

African American delegates at the General Conference voted overwhelmingly against the plan; white delegates approved it by a wide margin. After the Methodist Episcopal General Conference ratified the plan, it was sent to the annual conferences. Black annual conferences rejected the plan; however, the church as a whole sustained it. It was only as the black vote began to come in that some church people began to question the morality of pushing blacks into an arrangement they obviously didn't want.

During this time the southern church was not unattentive to the history being made north of the Mason-Dixon line. Silence on the matter of the plan of union was broken only as it became clear that the North was going to endorse it. While there was considerable support for reunion in the South, there was little enthusiasm for a united church with African American ministers and members, even if set apart in segregated structures. But finally, at their General Conference of 1938, the Methodist Episcopal Church, South, approved the plan. The Central Jurisdiction was the price for which, by moral compromise, the union of Methodists North and South was purchased.

Chapter Eight

Programmed Churches and Social Ferment

1939 to 1968

Throughout the decade of the 1930s there was a good deal of somber anxiety—banks failed, dictators prowled, wars raged abroad. Yet there were also moments of excitement and drama: abroad, a king abdicated to marry for love; at home, we had marathon dancing, alphabet soup, and permission once more to drink to it all. The most exciting moment for Methodists came in the spring of 1939 in Kansas City, Missouri: Three branches of American Methodism were at last united, forming The Methodist Church.

Seven years later, the Evangelical Church and the United Brethren Church joined to form the Evangelical United Brethren Church. A plan of union had been accepted by wide margins by the general conferences of the Evangelical Church in 1942 and by the United Brethren Church in 1945. Following the required approval, a uniting conference was held in the First United Brethren Church at Johnstown, Pennsylvania, in November 1946, to announce the birth of the new church.

Together, the two new churches included eight and one-half million members; their households made the community still larger.

Pacifism and Participation: World War II

As in World War I, so in World War II, there was a coalescence of piety and patriotism. Total war meant that the country fought with a moral passion that made her patriotism almost indistinguishable from her piety. By the eve of the war, Methodists, Evangelicals, and United Brethren had developed strong peace positions. The uniting conference of the Methodists in 1939 adopted a resolution "in opposition to the spirit of war now raging through the world." The spring of 1941 brought the nation and the churches one step closer to war, but the United Brethren General Conference continued to press for peace. Although making no attempt to bind the consciences of its individual members, the conference pledged itself not to endorse, support, or participate in war. Those who were conscientious objectors were promised the support of the church.

Within a few months after the conference adjourned, the nation was at war; the peace positions of the several churches would meet their toughest tests. Less than a year after Pearl Harbor, the Evangelical Church gathered for its General Conference and reaffirmed its prewar position that "war and bloodshed are not agreeable to the Gospel of Jesus Christ." It recognized the status of conscientious objectors and approved the office and ministry of military chaplains, but added that such action was "not to be construed as implying the endorsement of war by our church."

The second General Conference of The Methodist Church met two and a half years after the nation was officially at war. Could the Methodists in 1944 maintain their prewar stand, as the Evangelicals had? A majority report reaffirmed the pacifist position of 1939; a minority report blessed the soldiers, prayed for victory, and called for an all-out war effort. The clergy voted 170 to 169 in favor of the pro-war position, while the laity supported it 203 to 131—clear evidence of the long way Methodism had come in the years since World War I. The troubled conscience of Methodism on matters of war and peace was shared by United Brethren, who met for their last General Conference during the closing year of the war.

As the war dragged on, Methodists, Evangelicals, and United Brethren alike developed a sustaining conviction in regard to the need for a responsible world political organization. A "Crusade for a New World Order," initiated by Methodist Bishop G. Bromley Oxnam and adopted by the Methodist General Conference of 1944, was a model educational and action campaign that envisioned plans for the postwar world. Dialogue between bishops and political leaders in Washington was crucial to both sides. When American Protestantism in 1945 rallied behind the United Nations conference in San Francisco, the moral and political voice of the United States, in part at least, had been shaped by Methodism's crusade.

Programming Mission/Eliminating Racism and Sexism

With the formation of the Methodist and Evangelical United Brethren churches, there were continuing changes in polity and practice. The program boards proliferated and gained power and influence. Formal recognition was given to them in 1939, when Methodists created the Council of Secretaries to balance the Council of Bishops. Programs developed by the boards were adopted by the general and annual conferences and passed on to the people by bishops, superintendents, and clergy. Following two "successful" crusades (1944–1952), the idea of a quadrennial emphasis was written into the law of The Methodist Church in 1952, and a new board was created to promote future crusades—the Commission on Promotion and Cultivation. The "United Crusade" of the Evangelical United Brethren Church, 1954–1958, which brought in $5 million, was an example of the new church's program in action.

Racism

Methodists have long been involved in a struggle to eliminate racial barriers within and outside the church. Successive general conferences since 1939 had received increasing numbers of petitions for legislation on the issue symbolized by the all-black Central Jurisdiction.

Momentum to abolish the Central Jurisdiction increased in

the early 1950s, influenced by the attention given to the Supreme Court's school-desegregation decision of 1954. The first concrete step came at the 1956 General Conference, where more than four thousand petitions were presented on the race issue alone. The conference passed a forthright resolution condemning "racial discrimination or enforced segregation," established a churchwide quadrennial program on race and, most important of all, adopted legislation that would permit the transfer of African American local churches and annual conferences into the jurisdictions in which they were situated.

In the next eight years, however, only a few annual conferences and local churches transferred; by 1964, there were still seventeen black annual conferences. Pressure was building on both sides. Should the church enforce its resolution on race within its fellowship, or wait until each area of the country saw fit to take action? After a long and bitter debate, the General Conference of 1964 adopted a two-step plan to abolish the Central Jurisdiction. A deadline of September 1967 was set to transfer all black annual conferences into regional jurisdictions. Merging these annual conferences within their new jurisdictions became a mandate, and within a year, all had merged except those in the South. A special session of the General Conference in 1966 postponed the deadline.

In the meantime, union negotiations were coming to a head with the Evangelical United Brethren, which had a long history of strong antislavery sentiment and action. The plan that created The United Methodist Church in 1968 eliminated the Central Jurisdiction by failing to mention a jurisdiction based on race, but separate African American annual conferences continued on into the early 1970s. United Methodism's conscience was still troubled.

Sexism

In The Methodist Church, the issue of full clergy rights for women came up regularly at each successive General Conference. There was a flurry of excitement in the late 1930s when the plan of union was being drafted, that the new church would grant such rights to its women, especially since women already had such rights in the Methodist Protestant Church. But the uniting conference in 1939 failed to grant those rights by a close vote. Methodist women continued to press the issue at successive General Conferences, and the struggle for full clergy rights was finally won in 1956. The number of women ministers, however, did not swell; not till the late 1970s did women in increasing numbers test the commitment of the church.

While Methodist women gained a major victory in 1956, United Brethren women had been handed a severe setback at the time of union with the Evangelicals in 1946. Although the United Brethren had granted full clergy rights to women as early as 1889, and had a long tradition of women in their seminaries and pulpits, they agreed to follow the example of the Evangelical Church and give up the practice.

Ecumenism Family-style

In the nineteenth century, the word *ecumenical* signified the worldwide family of Methodist churches. But a Methodist layman, John R. Mott, changed all that in the early decades of the twentieth century. He was the one man, above all others, who gave impetus and organized direction to the ecumenical movement, and for this, he was awarded the Nobel Peace Prize; his living monument is the World Council of Churches.

Since 1900, few councils of churches or ecumenical projects have been without Evangelical, Methodist, and United Brethren participation. But by midcentury the churches were caught up in the tension of opposing forces—one pushing toward cooperation, if not union; the other pulling back from unreserved ecumenical commitment and possible surrender of precious traditions and institutions. This matter came to a head in the mid-1960s when the churches seemed to be heading in two directions at once. Both the Methodists and the Evangelical

United Brethren were members of the Consultation on Church Union (COCU) in the United States, in which nine American Protestant churches sought some form of visible church unity. At the same time, the World Methodist Council, formed in 1951 as a continuing secretariat between World Methodist Conferences, was pushing for the Methodists of the world to unite. The issue boiled down to "open versus closed" ecumenism. Failing to make a clear choice, leaders instead focused on expediting the Methodist/Evangelical United Brethren merger.

A scant ten years after the formation of the Evangelical United Brethren Church, it began to wind its way down the relatively smooth road to union with the Methodists. Formal discussions began in 1956. Ten years later, a plan of union had been readied for consideration by the two churches, meeting simultaneously in General Conference in Chicago. The constitution and proposed *Book of Discipline* favored the Methodist pattern on all important points of difference. As the conferences began to vote, it was clear that the delegates representing the two churches were very different in their attitude to union. Evangelical United Brethren delegates squeezed past the adequate number for approval by a mere fifteen votes, whereas the Methodists voted in favor of the plan by a huge majority. The next year, the respective annual conferences of the two churches ratified the plan with sufficient majorities. The United Methodist Church was about to be born!

Chapter Nine

Merger and Reappraisal at Midcentury

1968 to 1984

Lord of the Church,
We are united in Thee,
in Thy Church,
And now in The United Methodist Church!

With these words, Evangelical United Brethren Bishop Reuben H. Mueller and Methodist Bishop Lloyd C. Wicke announced the formation of The United Methodist Church to the uniting conference in Dallas, Texas, on April 23, 1968. That beginning, inspiring as it was, appears in retrospect more a grand pageant to mark the merger of two similar bodies than the creation of something distinctively new. That high moment of spiritual exultation was immediately followed by three quadrennia of dealing with an accumulation of issues that the drafters of the plan of union preferred to postpone. Part of the dilemma was the social trauma caused by Vietnam.

The United Methodist Church was born at a time when Americans were more divided than they had been for generations. The nation was in the midst of its longest and most troubling war. President Johnson's dramatic escalation of the war in 1965 sparked fierce debate. Some church people urged young men to resist the draft; others believed they had an obligation to serve their country in the armed forces. The morality of war troubled the consciences of United Methodists during this period and threatened to divide them once again. In the spring of 1972, when North Vietnam launched a major offensive with sharp gains in the south, President Nixon reacted by intensifying American bombing. Within weeks, United Methodists gathered for their first General Conference. Following a long debate the conference adopted a statement condemning the "immorality" of America's involvement in the war and called on President Nixon to halt the bombing. Within one year, a ceasefire was arranged, but the anger between pro- and anti-war church members remained.

Postponed Union Homework: Growing-together Pains

The ruling principle of the commission that worked out the 1968 Methodist/Evangelical United Brethren merger was "unite now, settle the differences later." Issues such as ministry and episcopacy, doctrinal standards and social principles, the number of seminaries, and a complicated cluster of national program boards, were not addressed. The uniting conference established a pattern of churchwide quadrennial study commissions to tackle them one by one.

The study that attracted most attention during the first quadrennium and at the 1972 General Conference was the report of the Structure Study Commission. There was widespread hope of the possibility of reversing the century-old trend of "one board after another," and even paring down the church's bureaucracy. In the end, the boards and agencies were merely grouped into four superboards—Church and Society, Discipleship, Global Ministries, and Higher Education and Ministry, with a simplified one-word description of each, respectively—advocacy, nurture, outreach, and vocation. The quota system for electing members created new and uncertain boards, but youth, women, and ethnic representatives gained a voice, while white middle-aged male clergy learned the consequences of sharing authority.

United Methodism, like any organized structure, bewails overlapping, duplication, and waste. The former Methodist Church had established a Coordinating Council to help the boards work together, but the council was never really effective. In the former Evangelical United Brethren Church, coordination was far more effective through a denominational Council on Ministries. In the united church, the Evangelical United Brethren structure was adopted, but debate continues on its effectiveness.

The 1972 General Conference continued the postponed union homework by establishing three study commissions of its own—one to study the seminaries, another to study ministry and ordination, and a third to study episcopacy and superintendency. Four years later, the reports came in. The general church accepted major responsibility for funding ministerial education, and the number of seminaries was reduced by one. New statements on "The Ministry of All Christians," the creation of a new Diaconal Ministry for full-time lay professionals, and an improved candidacy plan for ordinands resulted. The perennial question about whether district superintendents should be elected or appointed was resolved in favor of the appointed pattern. Life tenure for bishops was reviewed: Some argued that "term" episcopacy, the Evangelical United Brethren pattern, would encourage the election of bishops who would be relatively young or female or of ethnic background; others argued that limiting the term of bishops would only increase the power of church agency executives. Life tenure for bishops won, but their service as episcopal leaders in one geographic area was cut to a maximum of eight years.

Both Methodist and Evangelical United Brethren churches came to union in 1968 with strong statements on the social principles that guided their life and witness. The new church ended up with not one, but two statements of social principles—an aging Methodist Social Creed, adopted in 1908, and the Evangelical United Brethren "Basic Beliefs Regarding Social Issues and Moral Standards." Similar at some points, they were sufficiently different at others to raise questions about their theological and ethical foundations. Furthermore, the new church faced a new world situation; old problems were becoming more complex and difficult new ones had arisen. A quadrennial study commission was appointed by the uniting conference to resolve the matter. Finally, a fresh new statement of social principles and a new social creed for use in services of worship were adopted.

The new statement began with a call to responsible use of this world's natural resources. It gave vigorous support for birth control and limitation of population growth, as well as cautious approval to abortion and the remarriage of divorced persons. The right of responsible civil disobedience was recognized; support for conscientious objectors was extended to include opposition to particular wars. More explicit approval was given to the struggle for racial and social justice.

The statement on human sexuality was the most difficult of all to resolve. The study commission followed arguments from legal and medical professionals by recognizing homosexuals as "persons of sacred worth who need the ministry and guidance of the church" and whose "human and civil rights need to be ensured." But the conference voted with the people back home in affirming that the church does "not condone the practice of homosexuality" and considers it "incompatible with Christian teaching."

The Flowering of Caucus Methodism

When United Methodists gathered for their first General Conference in 1972, they found themselves struggling to understand what it means to be a pluralistic as well as a united church. Many were startled by the large number of persons wearing badges and buttons, handing out newsletters, holding press conferences, buttonholing delegates. The event marked the coming of age of United Methodism's growing family of unofficial caucuses—the racial/ethnic caucuses (African Americans, Asians, Hispanics, and Native Americans), along with women, youth, seminarians, and gays and lesbians. The sixty-year-old Methodist Federation for Social Action on the political left had been joined by the youthful Good News Movement on the political right. The time had come, each said in its own way, to redress the balance and discover the rich diversity of the United Methodist family.

American society had undergone tremendous cultural and social transformation in the 1960s. The rise of ethnic feeling indicated a renewed search for identity as well as a search for power. The United Methodist Church had a large and diverse racial and ethnic constituency, and it was being challenged to affirm the cultural differences of its people and allow them to express their faith in terms of their own life-style and cultural heritage.

The uniting conference of 1968 established a Commission on Religion and Race to promote the church's goal of developing a racially inclusive church. The 1972 General Conference made it a permanent commission with an expanded mandate. Since ethnic churches represent the area of highest potential for church growth or loss, the 1976 and 1980 General Conferences named the ethnic minority local church as one of the church's highest priorities.

Black Methodists for Church Renewal (BMCR), a national forum for black United Methodists, was formed in the midst of the civil-rights movements of the 1960s. Formally organized in 1968, the caucus avoided the call of militant leaders, both inside the church and out, to separate from the white church, and early announced its intention to work for change from within. By 1970 chapters were formed in all the jurisdictions and many annual conferences, and a monthly tabloid called *NOW* was being widely circulated. Over the next four years, BMCR chalked up an impressive record of achievements. It lobbied for the Commission on Religion and Race, urged church agencies to upgrade the level of African American leadership, and secured a General Conference commitment to raise substantial funds for

128

But Love and I had the wit to win: We drew a circle that took them in

Through the years many United Methodists have felt that Edwin Markham's words about a circle being drawn that shut a certain person out applied to them—women, African Americans, youth, Latinos, persons with handicapping conditions, Native Americans, children, Asian Americans, and others. Recently the excluded persons have taken the lead in enlarging the circle to take all persons in and give them places of responsibility in The United Methodist Church.

129

the church's black colleges and their students. By the early 1970s, however, BMCR had to share the spotlight with other groups.

United Methodism's most rapidly growing ethnic group is its Asian American community. Early in this century, Chinese, Japanese, Korean, and Filipino Methodist churches had been organized into separate annual conferences. In the postwar years, it was felt that Methodists of all ethnic and racial backgrounds should be united into one fellowship. Thus the Oriental Mission Conference, including Chinese, Korean, and Filipino churches, was dissolved in 1952. The Japanese Conference survived the terrible years of "relocation" during World War II and continued until 1964, when it merged with the California-Nevada Annual Conference. In recent years, however, many Japanese American United Methodists began to regret the loss of their identity and, together with Chinese, Korean, and Pacific Islanders, organized a National Federation of Asian American United Methodists to map strategy. A decisive early victory was the election of Wilbur Choy as bishop in 1972. In the 1980s, the caucus issued a call for the formation of a new Asian American conference.

Native American United Methodists, though small numbers are scattered around the country, are largely concentrated in Oklahoma, where they have been organized as an Indian Mission Conference since 1844. Eight thousand strong in 1990, they were led by forty ministers and four Native American district superintendents. The revival of American Indian culture led to the formation in 1970 of the Native American International Caucus (NAIC). Support for voting rights at jurisdictional and general conferences, efforts to raise educational standards and salaries of pastors, and communication among the fifty widely scattered churches outside the Oklahoma area have been NAIC's persistent concerns. A major resolution, "The United Methodist Church and America's Native People," stressing repentance and reconciliation, was adopted by the 1976 General Conference and revised and reissued by the 1980 General Conference.

Treated for decades as a stepchild of home-missions activity, the Latino churches in Texas, with the formation of The Methodist Church in 1939, achieved status as a separate Rio Grande Annual Conference, spreading over the lower Rio Grande River valley, with headquarters in the heavily Spanish-flavored city of San Antonio. The development of Latino American Methodism in the large cities on both coasts, as well as in the Southwest, runs counter to the tendency of other European ethnic ministries to merge with predominantly English-speaking conferences. A strong intention to maintain this visible distinction from the "Anglo" churches of the region is evident from the leadership of the national Hispanic caucus, Methodists Associated Representing the Cause of Hispanic Americans (MARCHA), formed in 1971. High on MARCHA's agenda from the beginning was the election of a Hispanic bishop.

The Commission on the Status and Role of Women (CSRW), created in 1970 and fully funded in 1972, was a second crucial new churchwide commission. Together with the United Methodist Women's Caucus, it kept women's concerns on the agendas of conferences and councils across the church. Women, no longer seeking careers in Christian education or mission but in the ordained ministry, began to enter seminaries in increasing numbers. By 1980 women represented more than 3 percent of the total professional ministry, an increase of 75 percent over 1975. While some local churches resisted the idea of a woman pastor, the appointment system did assure women employment in ministry. A few women were appointed district superintendent, beginning with Margaret Henrichsen in Maine in 1967; by 1980, the number had grown to seven. And a major breakthrough occurred that year when Marjorie Matthews was elected bishop.

Modern Methodism's oldest caucus, the Methodist Federation for Social Action (MFSA), highly suspect during the "red scare" of the 1950s, found new life and a new focus in the civil-rights and anti-war movements of the 1960s. Led by an energetic executive secretary, new annual conference chapters were formed, circulation of its *Social Questions Bulletin* doubled, and MFSA's long-standing critique of capitalism and support for organized labor were coupled with liberation theology and the promotion of boycotts of J. P. Stevens and Nestle products.

Highly visible and institutionally successful among the caucuses was the Good News Movement, which identified itself as a "Forum for Scriptural Christianity Within The United Methodist Church." Founded in 1966, Good News published a popular monthly journal, along with newsletters for women and seminarians, and information sheets on such issues as missions, church school curriculum, and legislative strategy. It sponsored large-group convocations and small-group think-tank meetings, "renewal groups" in the annual conferences, and had a major program aimed at making mission programs more evangelical. The caucus, which produced confirmation literature of its own, called on those responsible for church school curriculum to produce a track of distinctively evangelical literature.

Another caucus, the United Methodist Renewal Services Fellowship, a charismatic group formed as an outgrowth of the interdenominational Conference on Charismatic Renewal held during the summer of 1977, published a monthly newsletter, *MANNA,* and held national conferences to nourish Spirit-filled United Methodists.

A caucus of gay and lesbian United Methodists was organized. Following perceived homophobic actions at the 1972 General Conference, concerned clergy and lay members met at Edgehill United Methodist Church in Nashville to form a fellowship to educate the denomination about lesbians and gay men in the church. Organized at Evanston, Illinois in 1975, by early 1977 the caucus had taken the name Affirmation. It met twice yearly to map strategy, and published a newsletter to link members and friends. From the beginning, a principal goal of Affirmation was full laity and clergy rights for gay and lesbian persons in the church.

Theological and Liturgical Renewal

The doctrinal consensus of which Methodists, Evangelicals, and United Brethren boasted in the nineteenth century was badly shattered by twentieth-century theological fads. The result was a loosening of ties to the churches' theological traditions. In the post-World War II period, a few zealous Methodists, Evangelicals, and United Brethren tried to hold the old lines of fundamentalism or liberalism, but more and more, equally zealous persons came forward to advocate new theological fashions as they came along.

The churches' soaring optimism was severely tested by the successive tragedies of two world wars, the Great Depression in between, and the rise of communism, fascism, and Nazism. The liberal dream of a world becoming progressively better persisted, but the dreamers grew more anxious and less certain in the face of repeated disenchantments; this set the stage for a rebirth of interest in the One who stands above the tangle of human affairs. Divine initiative, human sin, revelation through Christ, and salvation by faith were newly fashionable under the label of Neo-orthodoxy. It was a great epoch in theology, but its direct impact on the churches was negligible.

In the 1950s, Christian existentialism, which stressed faith as a vivid personal experience, appealed to evangelicals who wanted to be modern. At the same time, a small cadre of Methodists was rediscovering Wesley, and the ecumenical movement was leading others to reconsider basic doctrines of church, ministry, and the sacraments.

The flare of hope aroused by the election of John F. Kennedy in 1960 called forth more radical theological options. The "death of God" hurrah and the flurry about the "Secular City" emerged and found their share of followers. A new interest in Oriental faiths led others to become devotees of Zen Buddhism and followers of itinerant Hindu gurus. By the 1970s, while evangelicals were reawakening and charismatics were feeling the Spirit, liberation theologies began to take center stage—black theology, feminist theology, third-world theology.

133

The constitution of The United Methodist Church, following the Methodist pattern, explicitly prohibits any alterations in "our present, existing and established standards of doctrine." The new *Book of Discipline* was full of procedures by which clergy and laity could be censured for teachings contrary to these doctrines. Yet nowhere were "our doctrines" defined, and scarcely anywhere were they understood. The joint committee on church union simply printed, back to back in the *1968 Book of Discipline,* the Methodist Articles of Religion, dating from 1784, and the recently updated Evangelical United Brethren Confession of Faith of 1962; the Judicial Council deemed them "congruent, if not identical in their doctrinal perspective and not in conflict." Yet they were not identical, and explicit references to the traditional Wesleyan foundations (Wesley's *Sermons* and *Explanatory Notes Upon the New Testament,* for instance) were absent from the plan of union.

As a result of this confusion, the uniting conference established a Theological Study Commission on Doctrine and Doctrinal Standards. It was assumed that the commission would prepare a new creed to replace the historic statements inherited from the former Methodist and Evangelical United Brethren churches. Sensing that such a course was doomed to fail, the commission formulated a new setting, into which the early faith statements were placed as foundation documents. Scripture, tradition, experience, and reason—all were recognized as theological guidelines. Diversity among United Methodist views was acknowledged.

The commission's report was adopted by the General Conference in 1972. United Methodism refused to become a creedal church and, instead, continued to set scripture, tradition, experience, and reason in interaction with one another as resources for shaping its theology. The report envisioned that church people would put theology on the agendas of all their conferences and councils, commissions and committees.

Liturgy

Two widely different styles dominated church architecture of the 1950s and 1960s—red-brick, white-pillared, tall-spired colonial, or clean-lined, natural-finished, A-frame modern. And widely different styles of worship were held in them. Major revisions of worship services occurred in 1959 when the Evangelical United Brethren Church revised its *Book of Ritual,* and in 1964 when the Methodists revised their *Book of Worship* and *Book of Hymns.* Sixteenth-century words and phrases dominated, since the revisions were essentially a recovery of inherited liturgies. Published on the eve of a decade-long movement of liturgical renewal, both churches were unable to take full advantage of the new insights which soon brought forth fresh liturgies from sister churches, Catholic and Protestant alike. Mid-sixties worship leaders, refusing to believe that recovery of past forms was the answer to making worship authentic and relevant, preferred to experiment with new forms of worship. So casual communions and chummy prayers, balloons and banners, guitars and folksongs, appeared.

To bring order out of chaos, in 1970 the newly united church authorized an Alternate Rituals Project. The proposed 21-volume Supplemental Worship Resources series was by far the most ambitious worship project in history. The new liturgies and worship resources were not designed to replace the service books of 1959 and 1964, but to give United Methodists more options. The first in the series, a new Lord's Supper service, was published in English in 1972, in Spanish in 1978, and in Japanese in 1982. In contemporary language, the service is not simply a revision of Wesleyan texts, but an attempt to follow classical and universal patterns. Fresh services of baptism (with confirmation and renewal possibilities) followed in 1976, and new wedding and burial rites appeared in 1979. Along the way, United Methodists traded the literary preaching of the early decades of this century for preaching based on a set of scripture readings for each Sunday; in many new churches, free-standing communion

135

tables replaced altars attached to the chancel wall; white robes and colorful stoles replaced the long-standing ministerial black.

New Ecumenical Ventures

To the flowering of United Methodism's long-standing caucus tradition and its attempts at doctrinal and liturgical renewal, participation in new ecumenical ventures was added in the late 1960s and early 1970s. The church took a giant step toward supporting Christian unity by adopting a major new resolution on "open" (versus "closed" or "family") ecumenism in 1968. The resolution acknowledged the gospel imperatives toward unity, and pledged United Methodism's continued participation in the ecumenical movement at all levels. Support for the National Council of Churches and World Council of Churches continued, despite criticism of certain (usually social) programs; enthusiasm for the Consultation on Church Union, a continuing plan to unite the major American Protestant denominations, waned. However, something new had appeared on the ecumenical horizon, and United Methodists were eager to join.

Bilateral conversations with Roman Catholics, on a national and international level, began in 1966. The purpose was to explore all that is held in common and to consider honestly the chief problems that separate. The conversations, which led to the publication in 1976 of a progress report titled "Growth in Understanding," included consensus statements on the Lord's Supper, ministry, and authority in the two churches. Interreligious dialogue with Jews was begun in 1972, and with Islam in 1980; inter-Methodist dialogue with the three independent African American Methodist churches was begun in 1979, and with other members of the Wesleyan family of American churches in 1980. In order to have a more effective ecumenical voice for and to the whole church, the 1980 General Conference created a separate General Commission on Christian Unity and Interreligious Concerns.

*Although the Methodist Episcopal Church
advertised its cooperation with the government's
war effort in 1917, the bishops of The United
Methodist Church, in their 1986 Pastoral Letter*
In Defense of Creation *said "a clear and
unconditioned NO to nuclear war and to any use
of nuclear weapons."*

Chapter Ten

Holding Fast/Pressing On

1984 to 1992

As the 1990s dawned in United Methodist-land, church leaders bemoaned the tough times, and many members felt depressed. Membership was down, morale was slipping, morality was slippery, mission was fuzzy. The distinctive identities of United Methodist and other mainline Protestant denominations had faded, and "brand loyalty" had weakened among churchgoers. What served individual needs took precedence over inherited ties to particular denominations. The element of choice came to affect not simply the way individuals related to congregations, but increasingly, the way congregations related to their denominational bodies. Congregations withheld full payment of "apportionments" (critics called them "taxes") to annual conference and general church agencies, and began to pick and choose which programs to support. This selective participation in denominational life made it difficult for denominational agencies to function and raised questions about their future.

Several key issues polarized Methodists and other mainline denominations. These included a perceived lack of biblical authority, an acceptance of new God-language, the advocacy of abortion and homosexuality, and a liberal leadership out of touch with a more conservative constituency. A growing conservative mood in The United Methodist Church and the diversity of its membership made living up to *United* difficult, if not impossible, to achieve.

HOLDING FAST/PRESSING ON (1984–1992)

Bicentennial Blues

American Methodism's bicentennial celebration in 1984 coincided with hemorrhaging membership. Bishop Richard Wilke sounded the first alarm in 1986 with his best-selling *And Are We Yet Alive?*; seminary professors William Willimon and Robert Wilson followed up with an equally hot-selling *Rekindling the Flame* the next year.

United Methodism's membership had peaked at more than eleven million in 1968, with the merger of the former Methodist and Evangelical United Brethren churches, but during the following twenty-five years, the numbers steadily declined. In the years between 1968 and 1990, membership dropped 20 percent, for a net loss of more than two million (11 million down to 8.8 million). Sunday school enrollment, traditionally the source of new recruits, plummeted even faster than overall membership. For two centuries *big and getting bigger*, United Methodists had to get used to the idea that they were big and *getting smaller.*

They were not the only ones singing the blues and wringing their hands. Other mainline Protestant churches suffered steep declines in the same period—Presbyterians (down 25 percent), Episcopalians (down 28 percent), and the United Church of Christ (down 20 percent). The plight of mainline Protestants might be understandable if all American churches were reeling from the shocks of secularism and the inroads of new faiths. But this is not the case. During the past two decades, African American denominations have gained, Roman Catholic membership has grown a solid 16 percent, and the boom in the conservative evangelical churches (including Fundamentalists, Pentecostals, and charismatics) has caused some to envision a religious revival.

Explanations for this shift abounded. Cultural and demographic changes eroded mainline churches, scholars said. Muffled messages, mumbled homilies, and misdirected voicings of the gospel failed to communicate the ways of God. Constant

139

organizational reshuffles took a toll. Preoccupation with political and social issues at the expense of good old-fashioned faith alienated many members. In addition, many of these churches lacked the marketing and communication savvy that evangelicals employed to win new members. However, a landmark study, *Mainline Religion in America* by sociologists Wade Roof and William McKinney, ended the 1980s on an encouraging note: Decline is not inevitable if churches will reclaim their spiritual heritage and take seriously their need to grow.

To stem the tide, The United Methodist Church's Council of Bishops, supported by the denomination's General Board of Discipleship, sponsored a church growth and evangelism event in the fall of 1990, for three thousand local-church lay and clergy leaders. The Fort Worth, Texas, "Gathering" combined training, inspirational worship, and major addresses by bishops, in an effort to encourage and undergird church-growth efforts across the denomination. A pastoral letter and study document by the bishops, *Vital Congregations—Faithful Disciples*, unveiled at the Fort Worth "Gathering," was read in local churches on November 18, 1990. The bishops' initiative provided congregations a time of "searching, self-examination, listening to God's word that they may see the new direction in which God is leading them."

The General Board of Higher Education and Ministry proposed a renewed emphasis on campus ministry for the 1993–1996 quadrennium. Data prompting the proposed emphasis were a 1990 Gallup survey which showed 55 percent of college students considered religion very important; increases in incidents of racial prejudice and abuse; and research showing that a high percentage of students went into ministry under the influence of campus ministers.

Doctrine: Back to Basics

Other initiatives aimed at conserving membership. Since The United Methodist Church is a big denomination made up of little churches, a task force proposed to the 1992 General Conference that ordained clergy who served churches with few members be allowed to supplement their incomes with other jobs, and that church organization be simplified to basic groups for nurture, outreach, and witness. The formation in 1992 of a church-wide committee on older-adult ministries helped the denomination focus on ministry to its graying members.

Not only were United Methodists failing to get their message across, they were increasingly unsure as to what their message was. Some complained that the 1972 doctrinal statement's endorsement of "theological pluralism" left United Methodists unclear in their beliefs, and in 1984, a General Conference committee began work to recast the statement. The committee's early drafts, in turn, stirred fears that the church was moving toward a new form of dogmatism. The new doctrinal statement made room for diversity and new currents of thought, however; but where the 1972 statement pointed strongly to assimilating new viewpoints, the 1988 statement emphasized the primacy of scripture and the richness of the United Methodist theological heritage.

After extended debate and redrafting in committee, the 1988 General Conference approved the revised statement by a wide margin (94 percent in favor). In the end, liberal church members were as happy as conservatives to reject the impression that "anything goes" in United Methodist doctrine. They responded positively, once amendments were added to ensure that the new statement was not endorsing any form of biblical fundamentalism, and to clarify that it encouraged church members to begin their theological reflection, not only with scripture, but also with their personal religious experiences and concerns about social injustice.

Doctrinal studies in the quadrennium 1988–1992 focused on baptism and ministry. Both generated considerable debate in the churches and at the General Conference. The commission studying baptism proposed to eliminate confirmation and establish baptism as the rite by which people join the church.

Baptized infants and children, the committee recommended, would henceforth be counted as full members.

The ministry-study commission's proposals to establish a consecrated lay deacon and eliminate the two-step ordination for elders sparked controversy. The new lay order of deacons would link worship to ministry in the world; candidates would acquire competence in a particular profession, such as church music or education, and complete religious studies. Deacons would become lay members of an annual conference. "Why fix what's not broken?" some United Methodist clergy and laity asked; others welcomed one or more of the recommendations to change ministry patterns.

What Shall We Sing? How Shall We Pray?

Next to the Bible, the church's hymnal shapes the way United Methodists believe and act. A sixteen-man, nine-woman committee, aided by a large number of readers, worked from 1984 until 1988 to prepare a new hymnal for United Methodists. Early in the process, word leaked out that the Hymnal Revision Committee would drop "Onward, Christian Soldiers" and use gender-inclusive language. After eleven thousand protesting letters, "Onward, Christian Soldiers" was retained, but "Strong Mother God" was dropped, and masculine imagery was restored to the proposed inclusive-language psalter. The revisers took greater liberties with texts that used masculine terms for humanity; not even works of Methodism's co-founder and greatest hymnodist, Charles Wesley, were spared. In his "Hark! The Herald Angels Sing," the line "Pleased as man with men to dwell" became "Pleased with us in flesh to dwell." In his "Christ the Lord Is Risen Today," latter-day Methodist "sons of men" no longer say Alleluia; instead, "Earth and heaven in chorus" say Alleluia. "God of Our Fathers" became "God of the Ages"; "Good Christian Men, Rejoice" metamorphosed into "Good Christian Friends, Rejoice."

While honoring traditional hymns, the 1989 hymnal shed the

142

elitism of past hymnals by making generous space for gospel songs, hymns from a wide range of ethnic groups, and contemporary hymns. Opting for popularity this time, the editors downplayed King James English and included songs that highbrows scorn but the people love, such as "In the Garden." The wide-ranging collection features such songs as the civil-rights anthem "We Shall Overcome," Duke Ellington's "Come Sunday," gospel singer Bill Gaither's "He Touched Me," and Brian Wren's "God of Many Names."

The overwhelming approval of the new hymnal by the 1988 General Conference was matched by an equally overwhelming approval in the parishes. More than half ordered the new book in the first year, and orders continued to pour into the church's publishing house. A separate Native American hymn and worship book titled *Voices,* the first ever for the denomination, containing folk parables, prayers, and gospel songs indigenous to more than twenty-five Native American tribes, was published in 1991.

New liturgies for baptism and communion, weddings and funerals, in trial use since 1972 and adopted by the 1984 General Conference, awaited the publication of the new hymnal for wide use. Their placement in the front of the new hymnal, along with a New Revised Standard Version psalter with musical responses in the back, began to change the way United Methodists worship and pray. Another change concerned the Lord's Supper. The Methodists specified in their 1966 hymnal that only "the pure unfermented juice of the grape shall be used." Teetotalers attending the 1988 General Conference failed to get that clause inscribed into church law, and the new hymnal omitted the rule, allowing congregations to use wine if they wish.

A United Methodist *Book of Worship,* designed for worship leaders, not for the pews, was prepared for presentation to the 1992 General Conference. Early agreements included adding resources for anniversary celebrations and the renewal of marriage vows, as well as services for reconciliation and healing after divorce or miscarriage.

143

Inclusive language sparked heated but fruitful debate about the nature of God and language about God throughout the 1980s. An *Inclusive Language Lectionary,* the first formal effort to eliminate exclusively male metaphors for God in the scriptures, was released by the National Council of Churches in 1983. The 1984 United Methodist General Conference followed this up with a report from the Task Force on Language Guidelines, which suggested that church members use fewer male pronouns in reference to God and look for alternatives to words such as Lord, King, and Father.

New Roles, New Power for Women

In 1972, 271 women had been ordained; in 1990 there were 4,200 women pastors. In 1972, 13 percent of delegates to the church's highest legislative body, the General Conference, were women; in 1988, 51 percent of lay delegates were women. In 1972, one clergywoman was serving as district superintendent; in 1990, 56 clergywomen had that leadership role. In 1972, the church had no female bishops; by 1988, five had been elected. One of those, Leontine Kelly, in 1984 became the first African American woman to be elected bishop in any mainline Protestant denomination. Further, the acceptance of women as pastors was growing. According to a 1988 United Methodist survey, more than two-thirds of 1,500 respondents believed that people in their congregations would accept a woman pastor more readily then than five years earlier. More than 70 percent saw no difference between the way women and men performed typical pastoral tasks.

On the downside, an African American woman was not appointed to the district superintendency until 1990, when three were appointed. Delegates to the 1988 General Conference narrowly defeated a petition to abolish the General Commission on the Status and Role of Women. The commission had been dogged by critics who charged that it had outlived its usefulness and had "expanded" its scope beyond the intent of its creators.

One of the most controversial actions was its support for a study of the effects of homophobia.

The church also struggled with the lasting impact of the sexual revolution. As women continued to strive for equality in society, churches confronted a vast array of issues—often tagged "family issues"—related to human sexuality: abortion; child care; sexual harassment; the trauma of divorce that leads to impoverished single-parent families headed by women; the difficulty of teaching children, teenagers, and adults how to respect and use human sexuality as a good gift from God.

Research on sexual harassment in The United Methodist Church by the General Council on Ministries in 1990 revealed that 77 percent of women clergy had experienced sexual harassment. Pro-Life advocates continued to challenge United Methodism's moderate position on abortion. Bowing to pressure, the 1984 General Conference altered the 1972 Social Principles statement to more clearly imply that The United Methodist Church considered "abortion on demand" morally wrong. As amended, the Social Principles continued to acknowledge "tragic conflicts of life with life that may justify abortion" and stated support of the "legal option of abortion under proper medical procedures."

Racial/Ethnic Presence

"Does anyone here have a Bible?" the Korean minister called out at the church social. From the back of the room, a Chinese layman raised a leather-bound book and waved it in the air. The Bible was passed gently over heads to the Korean, who opened it, stared wide-eyed into its pages, then let out a laugh. "It's in Spanish!" he cried.

With echoes of the Tower of Babel, in 1990, a disparate group of immigrants at Jackson Heights in Queens, New York, began to build an unusual United Methodist church. Every Sunday morning, prayers were said in four languages—English, Spanish, Korean, and Chinese—in separate simultaneous

145

services at the Community United Methodist Church. But unlike the Tower of Babel, which, according to Genesis, was thwarted by lingual diversity, Community Church thrived.

"We speak different languages," said one of the congregation's four pastors, "but we are one in Christ," and, he implied, one in The United Methodist Church.

The notion of different ethnic services under one roof—not unlike the multiplex movie theaters—grew, as they appeared in cities large and small across the nation. The multiple-congregation phenomenon became a strategy for ministry in changing neighborhoods. When the church in Jackson Heights was founded seventy years ago to meet the needs of European immigrants, it took the name Community Methodist Church. After it began to reach out to Chinese, Spanish, and Korean residents of its community, the church saw its membership double to four hundred.

Community Church in Jackson Heights, and others like it around the country, were exceptions. United Methodist attempts at a bold new mission among United States racial and ethnic communities failed in the 1970s and 1980s to yield significant results. From 1976 until 1988, Ethnic Minority Local Church (EMLC) was a missional priority of The United Methodist Church. Local congregations gave at least $20 million toward carrying out the mandate, and the money was used in many ways to strengthen racial/ethnic congregations. But only a small percentage of additional people were reached with the gospel and welcomed into the fellowship of United Methodist congregations. The nearly flat growth in racial/ethnic membership occurred during a decade of explosive growth in the racial/ethnic population. During this same period, while United Methodism was idling along, several other mainline Protestant denominations chalked up significant gains in racial/ethnic membership, notably the Baptists—American (northern) Baptists (up 43 percent) and Southern Baptists (up 70 percent).

Although racial/ethnic clergy made some gains in the United Methodist system, in 1991, pastorates in larger and more prestigious churches (most of them predominantly white), and high-profile, higher-paying positions, such as district superintendent and conference council staff, remained largely the domain of white males. Although the church's Judicial Council ruled in 1989 against mandated race and gender quotas for the governing boards of denominational agencies, those agencies were encouraged to give "special attention" to racial and gender inclusiveness.

African Americans

Through the denomination's years of priority attention to racial/ethnic churches, membership in African American churches dropped more than 1 percent, while the black population grew by 17 percent. Since the all-black Central Jurisdiction was dissolved in 1968, more than 140,000 blacks had left The United Methodist Church. By 1990, integration at the top-management level and in national church agencies had been achieved: There were ten active African American United Methodist bishops in the United States, plus nine more in Africa. A host of blacks served in staff positions across the church. Yet United Methodists lagged behind other denominations in developing older black congregations and organizing new ones. The "elevation" of able black pastors through the 1970s and 1980s, in retrospect, may have been at the expense of vigorous leadership at the congregational level. In 1991 the denomination had about 2,500 predominantly black congregations and about 244,000 black members.

For twenty-five years, Black Methodists for Church Renewal (BMCR) sought full participation for blacks in the life and leadership of the church by witnessing for justice and renewal through resolutions, legislative lobbying, confrontations with denominational and annual conference boards and agencies, and coalition-building with other groups. Yet progress was slight. By its own acknowledgment, BMCR was preoccupied with internal power struggles, self-maintenance, and playing it safe. With urban black communities savaged by drug abuse and violence, poverty, and despair, BMCR began to acknowlege that black

Methodists must discard middle-class complacency; set goals for church growth; go into troubled neighborhoods armed for guerrilla warfare; and put its faith into action to heal broken lives, to battle the destructive elements of the drug abuse, poverty, under-education, and disintegrating families that threaten the survival of blacks in the United States. Bishop Woodie White, a BMCR founder, summed up the predicament of blacks in The United Methodist Church by paraphrasing a familiar biblical text: "What would it profit us to save the black church and lose the black community?" He went on to say, "Not even slavery, horrible as it was, posed the threat that the black community faces today."

Still, there were bright spots. In 1968 The United Methodist Church formally abolished racial segegation from its structures; it took four years for South Carolina church members to follow suit and desegregate. Eighteen years later, in 1990, the South Carolina conference celebrated what, for many, was a bold stroke—the appointment of two black clergymen and three white clergymen in the conference's first cross-racial appointment to local churches. Bishop Joseph Bethea, the first African American bishop elected in the Southeastern Jurisdiction since union, made the history-making appointments.

Five times since 1979, bishops of the three predominantly black Methodist denominations—African Methodist Episcopal, African Methodist Episcopal Zion, Christian Methodist Episcopal—and The United Methodist Church have met to examine relationships and explore cooperative structures. At their spring 1991 meeting, the bishops moved to tighten their common ties of heritage and mission by authorizing a joint commission to study possible union.

Asian Americans

The brightest spot in the ten-year United Methodist effort toward racial/ethnic communities was seen in the Korean churches. The number of Korean United Methodists had been doubling every few years. More than half the United Methodist congregations established since 1981 were Korean, and their success stories became a blueprint to help reverse the denomination's otherwise plummeting membership. A national committee on Korean American ministries, under the auspices of the National Division of the General Board of Global Ministries, voted in July 1986 to establish Korean American missions in each of the denomination's five United States jurisdictions. By 1990, three Korean "mission superintendents" had been appointed to oversee new church development under the supervision of area bishops. The Korean success, however, was not duplicated among other Asian groups.

Hispanic Americans

The Hispanic community in America, after 1980, grew five times faster than the Anglo community. Yet Hispanic United Methodist churches grew by less than 3 percent, less than one-half percent each year. The total number of members did not exceed forty thousand. Such lack of progress in a time of significant growth in Hispanic communities across the land led Methodists Associated Representing the Cause of Hispanic Americans (MARCHA) to press for the election of a Hispanic bishop and the development of a national plan for Hispanic ministry. Bishop Elias Galvan was elected in 1984 and assigned to a newly created episcopal area in Spanish-tinctured Phoenix, Arizona. In response to MARCHA's request, the 1988 General Conference appointed a national Hispanic Ministries Committee to recommend a plan of action to the 1992 General Conference. Congregational development, clergy recruitment, deployment of lay missioners, and new missional structures to link widely scattered Hispanic churches, were high on the committee's agenda.

Native Americans

The contingent of Native American members is tiny, and in 1991 accounted for about 125 congregations and approximately

149

17,500 of the 8.8 million United Methodists. Their numbers declined by about 5 percent while the denomination was giving them and other racial/ethnic persons priority attention. That happened during a time of increases in the Native American population and soaring increases in the number of Americans who were identifying themselves as Native Americans.

In the middle 1980s, the Native American International Caucus (NAIC) drafted the first comprehensive plan *for* Native American ministries *by* Native Americans. Adopted by the 1988 General Conference and titled *The Sacred Circle of Life: A Native American Vision*, the plan impacted native people and The United Methodist Church through the development and implementation of: (1) a balanced theological approach sensitive to native cultural and spiritual values; (2) appropriate forms of worship, new modes of communication, and enhanced networking; (3) leadership programs in harmony with traditional leadership styles of native people; and (4) a national process to advocate the sociological, legal, economic, and political issues of native people. To remind the church of the contributions made by Native Americans, Native American Awareness Sunday was added in 1989 to the list of special days with offerings observed in United Methodist churches.

Sexual Hangups

Wide diversity and confusion marked church and society in the 1980s and 1990s on the issue of human sexuality, especially homosexuality. Bishops, pastors, and laity were not of a single mind in their understanding of the demands of scripture—particularly on issues of ordaining "self-avowed, practicing" gay men and lesbians and the blessing of faithful same-sex relationships. The early 1980s witnessed several test cases on the ordination and appointment of gay pastors. In 1982, Bishop Melvin Wheatley hit United Methodist headlines regularly after he appointed an openly gay pastor in Denver. Charges that

150

Wheatley's stance had undermined the authority of the Bible were filed by three Georgia churches. An investigative committee found no grounds for accusing the bishop, but the next year, a 3,500-member church in Colorado Springs "publicly censured" Wheatley, their bishop, for his active support of homosexual persons as ministers. Despite the strong language of the 1984 General Conference, which made it clear that no self-avowed, practicing homosexual person could be ordained or appointed as a United Methodist minister, debate on the status and role of gay persons in the church continued.

To "settle" the matter, the 1988 General Conference appointed and funded a major quadrennial study of the topic. The study committee gathered testimony from experts in theology, ethics, and the sciences, as well as attempting to give opportunities ("Listening Posts") for United Methodists at the grass-roots level to share their experiences. Interim reports showed the committee hopelessly divided on whether to lift the church's ban on ordaining practicing homosexuals.

The 1984 General Conference ban was a setback for Affirmation, the unofficial caucus for the interests of gay and lesbian United Methodists. Their stated goal was full laity and clergy rights for gay and lesbian persons in The United Methodist Church. In response to the 1984 ban, Affirmation launched a controversial "Reconciling Congregations Program" to encourage local churches and annual conferences to welcome lesbians and gay men into the full ministry of their organizations. By the early 1990s, fifty congregations, four annual conferences, and one general agency had committed themselves to hospitality, healing, and hope.

The worldwide pandemic of Acquired Immune Deficiency Syndrome confronted United Methodists with a challenge to reach out to people with AIDS. Criticized for their slowness in responding to that massive long-range challenge, an increasing number of churches, recognizing that laity, clergy, and even a bishop had died of AIDS, were beginning to speak out against

151

the AIDS stigma and to foster ministries that would support both people who live with—and die from—AIDS, and their loved ones and friends.

Bishops Take the Lead/General Agencies Recede

Since the revolt in the 1960s against imperial leadership styles, United Methodist bishops had been bound to an increasingly managerial job description. Charting the course of the denomination fell into the hands of the church's general boards and agencies. By the 1980s some United Methodists were begging the bishops to take back their leadership, and in the middle of that decade they began to do so. In 1986 The United Methodist Council of Bishops, following its Roman Catholic counterpart, issued an impressive pastoral letter on peace. Titled *In Defense of Creation: The Nuclear Crisis and a Just Peace,* the letter forcefully opposed nuclear war on religious grounds.

Four years later, in 1990, the bishops named one of their own, Bishop Felton May, to an unprecedented year-long special assignment in Washington, D.C., to provide concentrated leadership in the war on drugs and violence. At the year's end, Bishop May returned to his regular post, but continued to serve as a resource person for the Council of Bishops and as a liaison with United Methodist and ecumenical agencies to establish an "advocacy campaign to generate a more realistic governmental response to the national crisis." Several Methodist bishops took the lead in pressuring governments to impose economic sanctions against South Africa, as a way to end that country's policy of racial discrimination.

On the eve of the last decade of the millennium, a second major Pastoral Letter from the Council of Bishops dealt with church growth. Introduced before 3,500 United Methodists attending a late October 1990 "Gathering" in Fort Worth, Texas, the bishops called individual members and congregations to be "more intentional" in responding "to the command of our Lord to teach, baptize and to make disciples."

At the same time, the general boards and agencies and their staffs assumed a lower profile in the denomination. By the end of the century, The United Methodist Church had built up one of the largest private bureaucracies in the country, with hundreds of employees, several massive office buildings, and a denominational budget that approached $50 million a year in 1989. One-third of the church's *Book of Discipline* was devoted to their organization and responsibilities. At the same time, many United Methodists felt alienated from their church superiors.

Two factors colored the mood of alienation. First, some thought the agencies had shifted their focus toward involvement in areas of social change and away from service to local churches. An increasing amount of staff time and effort went into activities that either had their origin within the agency or dealt with broad issues in society. In both cases, such activities were the concern of only a small number of United Methodist people, and actually were opposed by some. The result was a waning sense of identification with the national program staff and their constituency, and vice versa.

A second factor lay in society's economic trends. The inflationary spiral during the 1970s and 1980s put severe pressure on many institutions, including churches. While giving to general church causes increased, it did not keep pace with inflation. In a time of economic stringency, the organization most distant from the source of funds is in the most precarious position. Most congregations meet local expenses first; denominational causes, no matter how worthy, are secondary.

The most severe critic of United Methodism's program boards and service agencies was the church's evangelical caucus, Good News. At the beginning of the 1980s, David Jessop, speaking for Good News, complained about financial contributions to "outside political groups" by the church's general agencies during 1977–1979. Roy Howard Beck's 1988 bombshell *On Thin*

Ice attempted to document that United Methodist national agencies leaned to the political left. He pointed to support for a "communist-dominated" conference that supported the liberation struggles of the peoples of South Africa. Beck also mentioned rumors about United Methodist leaders in Nashville and New York who were gay or lesbian, and he hinted that agency staffs in Nashville were deceitful and immoral. The Good News caucus gave wide publicity to Beck's charges and those made by Jessop.

In the wake of this heavy criticism and the fear of further alienating apportionment-payers back home, the general agencies began to take a lower profile in the denomination. The General Board of Global Ministries created a mission evangelism unit, partly in response to "evangelical" pressure. An Evangelical Coalition for United Methodist Women was formed in 1989 to counter what was seen as the Pro-choice stance on abortion and the missions-without-evangelism agenda of many nationally prominent United Methodist women.

Toward a Global United Methodist Church

In the early 1990s with more than one million members living outside the United States (800,000 members in Africa, 80,000 in Europe, and 60,000 in the Philippines), worshiping in four thousand churches led by three thousand ministers, The United Methodist Church continued to act like an American church. Some United Methodists at home and abroad longed for a new vision and a new structure that would truly embody John Wesley's vision of a world parish.

Three major factors sparked the move toward a global United Methodist Church in the 1990s. Perceptions and practices, including parts of the *Book of Discipline,* critics said, caused the denomination to operate as if it were merely a United States church, rather than a global church. United Methodists in conferences located outside the United States felt like second-

154

class citizens of the denomination because of isolating practices, such as "inviting" them to attend events as though they were not full members of the church, and not allowing them to participate in the financial support of the church by paying apportionments. Many leaders of autonomous Methodist churches in countries outside the United States said they would prefer to be United Methodists if they could link with the denomination and maintain their regional and cultural expressions of Wesleyan Methodism. A Bishops' Committee to Study the Global Nature of The United Methodist Church presented a plan of action to the 1992 General Conference. A preliminary draft of the plan recommended *one global* General Conference, *four regional* conferences (Africa, Asia, Europe, and North America), and *annual* conferences. Oversight would be provided by the Council of Bishops, already a global body, along with a global "program/mission agency."

The 1988 General Conference began to act like a global church when United Methodists accepted the proposal of the General Board of Higher Education and Ministry and pledged to raise $20 million during the following quadrennium to begin a United Methodist university in Africa. Located in Old Mutare, Zimbabwe, the Africa University opened in 1992 with colleges of theology, education, management, and agriculture. Additional colleges of humanities, medicine, and sciences were scheduled to appear later.

Two Parallel Denominations in One?

No one was surprised when a 1990 survey of United Methodist opinion by the church's General Council on Ministries found that "clergy were consistently more liberal than lay respondents" and that non-General Conference delegates were "consistently more conservative than General Conference delegates." Since the middle 1960s, two parallel denominations had developed within The United Methodist Church; alongside the liberal establishment, its conservative parallel grew up. By the middle

155

1980s, the church's twenty-year-old evangelical caucus, Good News, had its own seminary (Asbury Theological Seminary), its own publishing house (Bristol Books), its own bi-monthly magazine (*Good News*), its own Sunday school curriculum and confirmation manuals, and its own "annual convocation."

United Methodist evangelicals, sensing that their movement was on the upswing, became increasingly aggressive through the 1980s. In 1984, Good News launched an alternate Mission Society for United Methodists, to compete with the General Board of Global Ministries as a sending agency for Methodist missionaries. Its "Houston Declaration," issued just weeks before the 1984 General Conference and reportedly endorsed by 17,000 United Methodist pastors and more than 50,000 laypeople, swayed many General Conference delegates by its forthright condemnation of the ordination of homosexuals, its demand for the retention of traditional trinitarian language in liturgy, and its endorsement of the primacy of scripture.

Two years before the 1992 General Conference, Good News issued a bold prescription for Methodist reform: (1) enact membership requirements; (2) abolish guaranteed clergy appointments; (3) begin automatic four-year clergy appointments; (4) add lay people to boards of ordained ministry; (5) give laity a voice in the executive session of the annual conference; (6) bring back local preachers; (7) enhance consultation in the process of appointing pastors; (8) make apportionments voluntary; (9) highlight preaching and worship versus business at annual conference meetings; (10) make youth ministry a missional priority; (11) put the Ministerial Education Fund on a voucher system, so that funds would go directly to students, not to seminaries; (12) remove the trust clause, which prevents splinter groups from taking church property away from the denomination; (13) split the Board of Global Ministries; (14) retire the quota system; and (15) make the bishops lead.

Declarations issued by two Good News-sponsored convocations in 1990 (the DuPage Declaration and the Louisville Declaration) charged that United Methodism's problem was not faulty communication or flagging connectionalism, but apostasy. Both called upon United Methodists to confess the uniqueness of Jesus Christ as the only Savior, and to renew their dedication to world evangelization and holy living. Two centuries earlier, in 1786, John Wesley had identified the "constant doctrine" of the people called Methodists as "salvation by faith, preceded by repentance, and followed by holiness."

Conclusion

John G. McEllhenney

Our narrative reached the 1990s with the report, at the conclusion of the last chapter, that the Good News caucus had challenged United Methodists to acknowledge Jesus as the only Savior, recover holy living, and evangelize the world. Part One of this book opened with a description of the mission to Georgia undertaken by John and Charles Wesley in the 1730s. In between, more than two hundred fifty years of stirring and disturbing events marched past our eyes, marshaled by Frederick Maser, Charles Yrigoyen, Jr., and Kenneth Rowe.

To what purpose? Will knowledge of the past make us better United Methodists today? What is the point of studying history?

The point of studying history, according to Oxford University church historian Alister McGrath, resides in the fact that history reports on successful and failed experiments. By examining what has worked and what has not worked in the past, we can better evaluate what is occurring in United Methodism today.

As John Wesley evaluated Methodism in his day, he remembered what had happened to Christianity in the fourth century. Following the year 325, the Roman Emperor Constantine bestowed official recognition on Christian doctrine, lavished honors on Christian clergy, and showered riches on the cause of Christian evangelism. Christianity became, as a result, respectable, comfortable, successful . . . and slack.

When Wesley scrutinized fourth-century Christian slackness, he thought he saw a direct correlation between that and the fact that Emperor Constantine had made the church successful. The lesson he drew from history was that vital, pulsing spiritual movements cannot survive the crowning glory of success.

Success crowned Wesley's evangelistic efforts in the second half of the eighteenth century. The poor of Britain's shrinking rural hamlets and the outcasts of her burgeoning urban slums heard Wesley's good news of God's love for them in Jesus Christ. Listening to the gospel, and then yielding their hearts to God, they threw out their gin bottles, found jobs, and got a penny or two ahead on their bills. Those pennies piled up, making it possible for Wesley to take up collections. With that money, he purchased horses for his lay preachers, built preaching houses, and assisted those who were still poor, still out of work. They, in turn, began to work, save, and give. So as Wesley surveyed his Methodism, comparing it with what had happened to Christianity in the age of Constantine, he felt depressed by the signs of success.

Unlike twentieth-century Americans who believe that nothing succeeds like success, Wesley believed that nothing fails spiritually like worldly success. Was that, Wesley asked himself, what was happening to his Methodist people? Were they, like Christians in the age of Constantine, becoming rich in worldly things but slack in the spiritual?

Wesley had urged the Methodists to earn all they could, save all they could, and give all they could. But they took only his first two points seriously. Therefore they grew rich—not rich as twentieth-century Americans assess wealth, but modestly well-off; comfortable in their clean cottages; secure in having socked away a bit of money. In Wesley's view, even that moderate prosperity had sapped the very qualities that had enabled them to rise above their previous poverty—hard work, simple living, fervent faith.

Wesley, of course, set a different example, as we saw in this book's Introduction. As an octogenarian, he arose at 4 A.M.; endured storms at sea; preached at least once every day; maintained an extensive correspondence; argued about theology; made no secret of his detestation of slavery; and walked through streets "filled with melting snow" to collect money to buy clothes for the poor.

Even though Wesley's comment on the latter experience was that his "feet were steeped in snow-water nearly from morning till evening," he entertained no desire to settle down in a nicely furnished home, collect a pension, put up his legs by the fire, and bore visitors with his memories of the good old days. He always had more sermons to write and preach, more offerings to take, more people to rescue from the devil. And all because his Christianity crackled—crackled with the fires of salvation, crackled with a passion for telling others about his Savior's love.

The contrast between Wesley's restless yearning to be a knight errant of the gospel and the increasing readiness of his Methodist people to bask in their middle-class comforts, caused him to doubt the future of Methodism. The history of what had happened to Christianity in the fourth century, when Constantine made the church successful and rich, opened Wesley's eyes to the potential for spiritual failure of his increasingly successful Methodist movement.

"Wherever riches have increased," Wesley wrote in 1786 in his *Thoughts upon Methodism*, "the essence of religion, the mind that was in Christ, has decreased in the same proportion. Therefore I do not see how it is possible, in the nature of things, for any revival of true religion to continue long. For religion must necessarily produce both industry and frugality. And these cannot but produce riches. But as riches increase, so will . . . love of the world in all its branches."

Drawing upon historical accounts of how increasing wealth banks the fires of spiritual fervency, Wesley pressed home his fears for Methodism: "I am not afraid that the people called Methodists should ever cease to exist either in Europe or America. But I am afraid lest they should only exist as a dead sect, having the form of religion without the power."

This book provides materials for deciding whether Wesley's fears have come to pass, whether success has spoiled United Methodism; whether gloating over being a big church is one of the reasons United Methodism is a big church growing smaller. Has United Methodism become—like Christianity in the age of Constantine, like Wesley's fears for eighteenth-century Methodism—respectable, comfortable, successful . . . and slack?

CONCLUSION

Is The United Methodist Church similar to a middle-class person living in a tastefully furnished home, scanning the stock-market quotations for gains and losses, paying into a pension fund and dreaming of a retirement of reminiscing, glass of wine in hand, about the good old days when Sunday school enrollment ran high? Or does The United Methodist Church crackle with the spiritual fires of the age of Asbury, Otterbein, Boehm, and Albright? If that crackle has become an occasional dull snap, what will rekindle the flame?

Previous experiments with spiritual renewal can tell us what fails to ignite the fires of fervent faith—the official actions of established denominations! No Anglican council of bishops penned a pastoral letter that warmed John Wesley's heart and impelled him to become a force for Christian renewal in the British Isles and America. No Reformed general conference passed legislation authorizing Philip William Otterbein to meet with Martin Boehm at Long's barn to draw up a long-range plan for rekindling spiritual fires in eastern Pennsylvania. No think tank of Lutheran bureaucrats prioritized goals, voted evangelism number-one, and appointed Jacob Albright to be the super-bureaucrat in charge of saving souls.

History demonstrates that spiritual renewal comes through individuals who have received from God a word that breaks open minds and softens hearts. When such persons speak, others gather and respond to God's love. These new believers, having gathered once to hear fresh good news of God's love in Jesus Christ, continue gathering to nurture the growth of that love in their lives and in the world around them. Gradually, almost imperceptibly, these newly minted followers of Jesus become, without any strategy formulated by a denominational task force on spiritual renewal, glowing coals of new faith in a bed of dying spiritual embers.

For church leaders, the problem posed by glowing coals of faith is whether to poke them closer to the dying spiritual embers, or douse them with buckets of bureaucratic cold water. Expressed in less colorful terms, do church leaders welcome spiritual renewal wherever it bursts into flame, applying only the Gamaliel test—"If this plan or this undertaking is of human origin, it will fail; but if it is of God, you will not be able to overthrow" it (Acts 5:38-39 NRSV)? Or do church leaders stifle any spiritual renewal that has not been devised by their committees and approved by a majority vote of their conferences?

History reports that church renewal does not come from official actions, but from surprising divine intrusions. Nothing essential has changed since the coming of Jesus. He appeared as the Messiah in the midst of a community immersed in messianic expectations. But he was too much of a divine surprise for the leaders of that community to welcome him.

Is United Methodism today a Christian community capable of rejoicing in a bonfire of the Spirit? Would its leaders welcome flaming tongues like those of John Wesley, Harry Hosier, Francis Asbury, and Frances Willard? Could United Methodism's bishops welcome new Otterbeins and Albrights, while holding them accountable to the fullness of Christian doctrine and freeing them to communicate that doctrine in fresh ways? Is contemporary United Methodism hospitable to the burning passion that kept Wesley on the move for Christ, even at age 84?

No historian can predict what would occur if a new Wesley were to appear on the United Methodist scene. The authors of this book can say only, "Study the past and learn about previous experiments with spiritual renewal." What we learn will make us better United Methodists—better, because we shall be alert to the possibility that God is about to commit spiritual arson in our church.

Bibliography

Ahlstrom, Sydney E. *A Religious History of the American People.* New York: Doubleday, 1975. 2 vols. Paperback. Helps set United Methodist history in its larger American context.

Behney, J. Bruce, and Paul H. Eller. *The History of the Evangelical United Brethren Church.* Nashville: Abingdon Press, 1979. The standard history of Evangelicals and United Brethren from their beginnings through union with Methodists in 1968.

González, Justo L., editor. *Each in Our Own Tongue: A History of Hispanic United Methodism.* Nashville: Abingdon Press, 1991. Paperback. A survey of Hispanic United Methodist history in the five jurisdictions and Puerto Rico.

Guillermo, Artemio R., editor. *Churches Aflame: Asian Americans and United Methodism.* Nashville: Abingdon Press, 1991. Paperback. Tells the story of Asian American United Methodists and their involvement in the denomination's development.

Langford, Thomas A. *Practical Divinity: Theology in the Wesleyan Tradition.* Nashville: Abingdon Press, 1983. Paperback. Traces the development of Methodist theology from Wesley to the middle of the 20th century.

Noley, Homer. *First White Frost: Native Americans and United Methodism.* Nashville: Abingdon Press, 1991. Paperback. Narrates the history of Native American United Methodist peoples.

Norwood, Frederick A. *The Story of American Methodism.* Nashville: Abingdon Press, 1974. The basic survey.

Shockley, Grant S. *Heritage and Hope: The African American Presence in United Methodism.* Nashville: Abingdon Press, 1991. Paperback. Clearly written basic survey of the historic participation of African Americans in United Methodism.

BIBLIOGRAPHY

For Further Information

Susan M. Eltscher, ed. *Women in the Wesleyan and United Methodist Traditions: A Bibliography.* Madison, N.J.: General Commission on Archives and History of The United Methodist Church, 1991. Paperback.

C. Jarrett Gray, Jr., comp. *The Racial and Ethnic Presence in American Methodism: A Bibliography.* Madison, N.J.: General Commission on Archives and History of The United Methodist Church, 1991. Paperback.

Kenneth E. Rowe, comp. *United Methodist Studies: Basic Bibliographies.* Nashville: Abingdon Press, 1992. Paperback.

Index

167

INDEX

Poverty, 48f., 70, 100f., 159f.

Prayer meetings, 48, 74

Preachers/pastors, 71f., 75, 80, 92, 112, 113, 136, 140f., 144, 146f., 155, 156

Primitive Methodist Church, 57

Program boards, 120., 125f., 138, 140, 152ff., 155, 156

Publishing, 35, 53, 56, 61, 75, 78f., 85, 90, 91f.

Quarterly Conference, 60

Quota system, 125, 147, 156

Racial/ethnic concerns, 98f., 110f., 120f., 125, 128ff., 145ff.

Rankin, Thomas, 34, 35, 38

Reception of members, 47f.

Renewal, spiritual, 161ff.

Republican Methodist Church, 57f.

Revivalism, 62ff., 69, 99f.

Sacraments, 13f., 35, 39ff., 42, 45f., 72

Shadford, George, 34, 35

Shaw, Anna Howard, 96

Slavery, 15f., 24, 44, 55, 59, 70, 81ff., 86

Social concerns, 55, 69f., 81, 86, 99ff., 107f., 126f., 140, 153

Social Creed/Social Principles, 101, 126f., 145

Social Gospel, 100f.

Societies/small groups, 12, 23f., 72

Stewart, John, 61, 77

Strawbridge, Elizabeth, 29f.

Strawbridge, Robert, 28, 29

Sunday schools, 56f., 75, 92, 139

Thorne, Mary, 36

Union Church of Africans, 60

Union of churches, 53, 61, 85, 90, 103, 114ff., 118, 121, 123, 124

United Brethren, 26-28, 36, 39, 51, 53ff., 60f., 65, 69, 72f., 81f., 94, 96, 98f., 118, 119

United Methodist Church, 121, 123, 124, 125ff., 128, 134, 148

United Methodist Renewal Services Fellowship, 132

War, attitudes toward, 37f., 55, 106f., 118ff., 124f., 127, 152

Wars
American Civil, 86f.
American Revolution, 37ff.
Vietnam, 124f.
World War I, 107
World War II, 118ff.

Watch Night services, 48, 74

Webb, Captain Thomas, 28, 30, 31, 34

Wesley, Charles, 13f., 18, 20f., 22, 62, 142, 159

Wesley, John, 9ff., 20f., 22-25, 26, 27, 31, 33, 34, 35, 37f., 41, 43, 53, 55, 56, 62, 78, 79, 82, 86, 93, 112, 134, 154, 157, 159ff., 162, 163

Wesleyan Methodist Church, 83

Wheatley, Bishop Melvin, 151

White, Bishop Woodie, 148

INDEX

Whitefield, George, 21f., 23, 25, 26, 30
Wilke, Bishop Richard, 139
Willard, Frances E., 95, 100, 163
Women, 36, 56, 70, 78, 95f., 98, 111, 121f., 128, 131, 144f.
Women preachers, 15, 96, 111, 121f., 131, 144
Worship, 13, 29, 36, 42, 45ff., 60, 62, 72, 73ff., 92f., 105, 112f., 135f., 143, 145f., 156
Wright, Richard, 33

Youth, 125, 128, 156

Made in the USA
San Bernardino, CA
29 August 2014